Secrets in the Dirt

Secrets in
the Dirt

*Uncovering the Ancient
People of Gault*

Mary S. Black

Texas A&M University Press
College Station

This paper meets the requirements of ANSI/NISO Z39.48–1992
(Permanence of Paper).
Binding materials have been chosen for durability.
Manufactured in China through FCI Group

Library of Congress Cataloging-in-Publication Data

Names: Black, Mary S., 1946– author.
Title: Secrets in the dirt: uncovering the ancient people of Gault / Mary S. Black.
Description: First edition. | College Station: Texas A&M University Press,
   [2019] | Includes bibliographical references and index. |
Identifiers: LCCN 2018047508 (print) | LCCN 2018049737 (ebook) | ISBN
   9781623497507 (ebook) | ISBN 9781623497491 | ISBN 9781623497491
   (flex with flaps: alk. paper)
Subjects: LCSH: Gault Site (Tex.) | Clovis culture—Texas—Bell County. |
   Antiquities, Prehistoric—Texas—Bell County. | Excavations
   (Archaeology) —Texas—Bell County. | Bell County (Tex.) —Antiquities.
Classification: LCC E99.C832 (ebook) | LCC E99.C832 B55 2019 (print) |
   DDC 976.4/287—dc23
LC record available at https://lccn.loc.gov/2018047508

*All illustrations are courtesy of the Gault School of Archaeological
Research (except as otherwise indicated).*

Contents

Acknowledgments

My gratitude goes to Michael B. Collins and Clark Wernecke for generously encouraging me to join this project. They gave me access to all field journals, maps, notes, and other documentation of the Gault archaeological project as I tried to write this story. Mike and Clark, along with other members of the staff of the Gault School of Archaeological Research (GSAR), patiently answered all my questions as I tried to understand the complex endeavor of recovering and interpreting evidence from the distant past at this particular place. Clark toured me around the site one fine day in spring before everything was backfilled so I would have an idea of setting and logistics. David Olmstead kindly allowed me to interview him, and showed me a cast of his discovery of the "hot dog in a bun" that set off twenty-five years of archaeological investigation.

I could not have accomplished this work without the support of my archaeologist husband, Steve, who saved me over and over. In addition to Steve, who read numerous versions of this manuscript, I also want to thank Al Weslowsky for helping me think though the earliest stage of planning, and Alston Thoms for his insight into historic Native American groups in Central Texas. I also thank Kenneth M. Brown for his clarifying comments on the manuscript, and Anna Jaworski, who read an early draft and visited the fine exhibit on Gault at the Bell County Museum with me.

Robert Lassen, Sergio Ayala, Jennifer Gandy, Tom Williams, and Nancy Williams from the GSAR staff allowed me to follow them around and ask questions without the least hesitation. Bruce Bradley and Dick Boisvert, among others, made me laugh with their stories. Marilyn Shoberg, Erin

Keenan-Early, and Laura Vilsack shared insights from their research with me. Jon Lohse, James Beers, Sharon Dornheim, May Hamilton Schmidt, Pam Wheat Stranahan, Jonelle Miller-Chapman, Doris Howard, and Bryan Jameson contributed their thoughts and experiences to help me understand the day-to-day effort of uncovering the detritus of life gone by. Charles Frederick helped me understand various archaeological dating methods. To each of them I owe my sincere thanks. More than 2,300 people were part of the Gault project in some way, and I could not possibly interview all of them. For those I have overlooked, please accept my deepest apologies. Your contributions are greatly appreciated. Understanding the ancient people of Gault has been, and continues to be, a product of many people working together to unlock the human past.

A Note on Spelling and Writing

Modern English being the mongrel that it is, there are two correct ways to spell *archaeology*, or *archeology*. Using the "ae" in the middle is the older way, coming from seventeenth-century French by way of Latin and Greek, and the simplified "e" is supposed to be more contemporary. But archaeology is not a contemporary field of scholarship. Indeed, the discipline is dedicated to antiquity. Therefore I have used the "ae" version of the word in most places in this book. Some archaeological associations prefer the modernized "e" spelling in their names, however, perhaps to distinguish themselves as strictly American. Thus readers will see both spellings in this book—I just hope I got them in the right spots!

This is a book of nonfiction. However, I made up the prehistoric vignettes that introduce certain chapters. Human conversation, emotion, and beliefs from such ancient times simply cannot be conveyed any other way. Thus fiction serves to connect modern people in a personal way to the evidence of a past that science is only beginning to explain.

Names for the fictional prehistoric characters were selected from various Native American names from different tribes during historic times. The names themselves are not accurate to the ancient time periods of Gault, however, because researchers know very little about the languages spoken thousands of years ago. By using Native American names, however, I tried to give at least some flavor of ancient North America.

Secrets in the Dirt

1 Old as Dirt

There is a place in Central Texas where the dirt is giving up its secrets. It's a lovely little spot set along the banks of spring-fed Buttermilk Creek. Shaded by tall bur oaks and pecans, the alluvial bottom is considerably cooler that the rocky uplands fifty feet above. Situated where the Texas Blackland Prairie and the Edwards Plateau come together, the location has easy access to plants and animals of two different bioregions and offers a genial place to live.

The place is known by archaeologists as the Gault site, where people first left behind reminders of their lives on the ground around sixteen thousand calendar years ago. (All dates in this book refer to calendar years.) But soon everyone may know it as a spot where some of the earliest human beings on the North American continent resided thousands of years before that, pushing back the timetable for the arrival of people in North America. This book seeks to give an understanding of the people who lived and worked in this location over the millennia and the significance of the materials they left behind.

More than 2.4 million artifacts have been recovered by archaeologists and citizen scientists at Gault. The artifacts found at Gault represent the full range of the known stone tool technology from the region. They also expand the range, with several unique specimens known from nowhere else as of yet. To clarify, an artifact is anything made or modified by human beings: A notebook is an artifact, and so is a car. So is a spearpoint made of stone or a flat rock engraved with symbols. An apple is not an artifact, but a rib bone with marks from butchering with a knife is. If human beings modify a naturally occurring resource, such as stone or bone, to make something useful or meaningful to themselves, they are making things that archaeologists call *artifacts*. The Gault location covers more than sixty acres, making it one of the largest reservoirs of artifacts from the Clovis cultural period ever discovered. Plus there is significant evidence for human occupation in this place that is older than that. In other words, Gault is a huge repository of evidence of early humankind in North America.

The Gault archaeological site has been more or less continuously occupied for more than sixteen thousand years. For contrast, Damascas, considered the oldest city in the world, has been occupied about eleven thousand years. But the story of Gault is not told by buildings, treasure, or written documents like the history of Damascas. The story of Gault is told by the dirt.

Literally thousands of people worked together at Gault over twenty-six years to uncover this story. The story of Gault is not only remarkable for the evidence discovered there, but also for how the discoveries were made. Many were made by citizen scientists, working on weekends, unpaid. More than 2,300 such individuals worked intermittently at Gault over the years to recover new information about the human past. By collaborating with professional archaeologists, these interested amateurs helped gather evidence that writes new chapters in the history of the Western Hemisphere. Overseeing this hive of activity was archaeologist Michael B. Collins, who directed the project with vision.

Before Collins arrived on the scene, the banks of Buttermilk Creek had been dug into for more than seventy years by hobbyists hoping to find a perfect arrowhead for their collection. The landowners charged a nominal fee per day to dig. Hillocks of dirt had been shoveled into rough mounds all along the creek. But none of the afternoon adventurers ever dug down very deep, which is fortunate for our story.

Here's how it all happened. How the artifacts may have gotten there, who probably made them, who found them, and what it all means for you and me.

Imagine, if you will, once upon a time . . .

13,300 Years Ago

An old woman stroked a stone in her hand as she had so many times before. "Oh Mother of All Life, bless us with your flowing water," she prayed. "You sustain us. You give us life. Be here for us all our days, and the days of our grandchildren's grandchildren."

She traced the sinuous line the old shaman had engraved like a snake down the middle of the stone.

"This is my birthing stone. It protected me well and saved me from birthing death so long ago. Now I give this stone to you, to protect our band. Keep your water bubbling in the spring. Do not let Father Sun win his battle over you. Keep strong, that you may give us life."

She gently laid the powerful stone face up into the cool mud.

"Take also this ancient blade from Takoda. He put his breath into this spearpoint long ago that it might protect the forces of life." She nestled a worn blade of creamy chert streaked with pink on top of the snake stone.

"And last this from Neka, who has joined the spirits." The old woman carefully placed a second stone about the size of her palm on top of the blade, covering it like a finely worked hide. Then she sealed the gifts away in a little hole she had scooped out near the spring, patting damp soil and moss over them.

"With these offerings, we praise you Oh Mother of Life, Mother of Living Water, Mother of the Spring. Remember us, your people."

The young man used his day off to have a little fun in the dirt. David loved the vigorous work of digging holes and combing through back piles to find discarded treasures. He already had a bucket full of nice projectile points, sharp tips for darts or arrows, when he broke through a yellowish, sandy layer that stood out from the black dirt in the upper part of the hole he was in. He brushed the crumbling soil away and saw the ends of two stones sticking out in the wall of the pit, one atop of the other.

"That's funny," he said to himself. Most of the points he found were scattered casually here and there, but these two stones looked like they had been deliberately set on top of each other. He threw down his shovel and pulled the first one out of the wall. "Well, I'll be darned."

The rock had strange, unnatural lines drawn on it, like little squares. He reached up again and pulled out a short, broken stone tool, and then another flat rock underneath it.

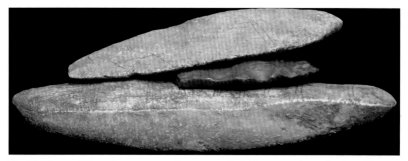

David Olmstead found two engraved stones sandwiching a much-used point. The plastic replica shown in this photo is realistic except for the coloring of the chert point, which was creamy white striated with pink.

"Whoa, what's all this?" he asked himself under his breath. "They look just like a hot dog in a bun," he exclaimed as he looked at the two stones that had sandwiched the stone tool. The point was smooth, flaked stone, creamy white striated with pink, an unusual color for around here. The bottom stone had faint lines carved on one side, with one long curving horizontal line. Two engraved stones together with a beat-up chert point. He'd never found anything like that before. He sat back on his heels for a minute as he contemplated his next move. Then he quickly wrapped up his

Point, Blade, or Knife?

Archaeologists classify stone tools by both form and function. For example, a carefully shaped and thinned pointed tool made by chipping or flaking on both sides is called a "point" or "projectile point." These are often used for stabbing or piercing, such as a spearpoint. A "blade" is a long, narrow, thin flake of stone made by striking a prepared stone cobble, or core, with a hammer made of stone or antler. Blades are not flaked, but have long, straight, more or less parallel edges. They may be used as tools themselves, or they may be further shaped into specialized tools. "Knives" are sharp, thin stone tools fitted with wooden or antler handles and used for slicing or scraping. Other types of stone tools are made of ground stone rather than flaked, such as manos and metates.

finds in an old rag, loaded up his tools, grabbed his bucket, and headed to the car.

"Had enough for one day?" another digger called.

"Oh yeah," David yelled. He'd had enough all right, but he dared not show the others what he'd found. David Olmstead, an arrowhead enthusiast, had spent many afternoons burrowing around the old farm. Like many others, he paid the farmer twenty-five dollars a day to dig holes in the ground near the creek.

David drove home that evening excited about what he'd found. He couldn't wait to get home and examine the markings on the rocks under a good light. He knew his finds would be valuable on the arrowhead collector market, but he didn't know how scientifically important they really were.

Since that day in 1990, professional archaeologists and volunteer citizen scientists have recovered more than two million artifacts near the small stream now known as Buttermilk Creek. The Gault archaeological site has yielded many stone tools and broken bits that seem to be between thirteen and sixteen thousand years old. Because these remains are so old, and because there are so many of them, the site has caused researchers to question assumptions about our nomadic ancestors. Moreover, views about the intelligence, creativity, and problem-solving abilities of people from thirteen thousand years ago or more are being revised upward. Human beings, it seems, may be smarter than we look. And we may have come to the Americas long before anyone previously believed.

The farm where David was digging took its name from the man who owned the place in the early 1900s, Henry Clay Gault. Today walnut trees still grow tall by the shallow stream. Oaks, pecans, and a dozen other hardwoods sink their roots deep into the rich, well-watered soil, creating a lush and shady place. Chert still juts out of the slope on one side of the stream, and can be found easily on the ground. Many pieces are as big as a fist, and some the size of small watermelons. A low bluff rises about forty-five feet to the uplands where thin soil and bare stone support a few stunted junipers, mesquite, and prickly pear. Beyond the stream valley, almost everything changes dramatically in only a few miles—the plants, the animals, the contours of the land, and the soil itself.

People found this location advantageous for thousands of years. When available, they could hunt buffalo and antelope in the tall grasses of the

Buttermilk Creek flows under shady trees in Central Texas where two ecotones join, providing a variety of plants and animals.

nearby prairie and deer and turkey in the rugged hills. Multiple plant communities provided a great variety of grasses, wild fruits like persimmons and prickly pear tunas, and medicinal herbs. They had water, and nut trees, and material for making baskets. And chert for tools. The whole range of natural resources they needed was available right here.

Today rock is still important, and eight limestone quarries line the paved county road in front of the property for several miles. There are three rock quarries within a thousand feet of the gate at Gault. Trucks haul tons of limestone from these quarries to building sites and wholesalers all over the county. The loud, constant rumble of the quarries crushing stone and cutting it into slabs for houses and patios continues day and night. All this is located about forty miles northwest of Austin, Texas, near the small town of Florence, and not far from David's house. It was an easy drive for him to come out to his digging spot for an afternoon.

The property has changed hands several times since that day, and is now owned by the Archaeological Conservancy, a nonprofit organization dedicated to protecting endangered locations of the human past. Gault is an exceptionally good place to study human behavior over the years because it has been more or less continuously occupied for almost eight hundred generations (saying a generation equals twenty years, divided into sixteen thousand years).

Evidence from the Gault archaeological site is challenging the idea that people managed to walk from Siberia across the Bering Strait, through a relatively narrow corridor between two massive glaciers in what is today Canada, to spread throughout North America and part of South America in only five hundred years. Only a few years ago, Ice Age people were also imagined to have hunted mammoths and other late Pleistocene animals to extinction, while somehow populating an entire continent as they went.

Granted our human forebears were smart and brave in many ways, but it's doubtful they could have walked all the way from Siberia to South America and colonized from the West Coast of North America all the way to the East Coast in only five hundred years. For example, Gault is helping us understand that early Americans knew their local environments extremely well, a task too complex for nomads rushing by as mammoths stampeded. The ancient people at Gault knew where to find the best stone for making tools, rather than just using the nearest source. They cached ready-made tools and preformed blades at certain places, presumably planning to return. They made art of various kinds, although for what purposes we do not know. If they were running after the herd, would they stop to do that? And they relied on small game like rabbits, lizards, and turtles for dinner most of the time, instead of constantly feasting on mammoth haunch.

The Gault archaeological site is one of the largest sites from the Clovis cultural era (about a 600-year span approximately 12,900 to 13,500 years ago) ever found. The vast majority of artifacts archaeologists have found there are from this time period. This is amazing in itself. The huge amount of material allows archaeologists to learn more than ever before about everyday life so long ago. "Gault is one of the sites that has started to reveal Clovis life to us. It was just a hub of activity," explained archaeologist Robert Lassen with the Gault School of Archaeological Research.

The Gault site is the largest Clovis-era manufacturing workshop ever found, at least in terms of the number of artifacts. At least nineteen complete Clovis spearpoints have been found, all showing signs of wear and resharp-

Some of the Clovis projectile points recovered from the Gault site by Mike Collins and his crew. Most show signs of wear and breakage.

ening by ancient hunters. A number of Clovis point fragments, often just snapped at the tip, have been discovered. If these broken points are included in the count, then there are about 40 Clovis points all together. In addition, at least 139 incised stones have been revealed. A solitary broken tool made of bone was also recovered, and a mysterious formation of small cobblestones. Perhaps thousands of small, broken, poorly preserved bone pieces add to the list of recovered items. All the rest—thousands and thousands of artifacts— is debitage, or chips of chert from making tools, or other intentionally broken pieces of stone.

But resting on the bedrock, below the Clovis flakes and tools, was a big surprise. In soil that had not seen the light of day for more than sixteen thousand years lay stone implements that were clearly shaped by human hands but showed no influence of the Clovis cultural design. They were older than Clovis. As old as the dirt itself.

Thousands of ancient people left reminders of themselves at Gault for thousands of modern people to try to reconstruct. More than three hundred members of the Texas Archeological Society (TAS) came one year. Another

Enthusiastic volunteers and students from many places worked at Gault over the years to meticulously excavate delicate artifacts.

forty-six volunteers came from the Tarrant County Archeological Society (TCAS) one weekend. Another time, twenty-seven Boy Scouts and thirteen adult leaders came as part of archaeology merit badge activities. Mike Waters and Harry Shafer of Texas A&M University trained a field school group one year. Eighteen students from Brigham Young University led by Joel Janetski earned field school credits during another summer. These were dedicated people. As Joel used to say, "If you're not thinking about archaeology, you're wrong." A lot of people have thought a lot about the archaeology at Gault, and they are beginning to understand the clues.

Stan Ahler, former director of the PaleoCultural Research Group, brought a group of eleven who put in 684 hours working 9-hour days. In 2000 Dick Boisvert from the New Hampshire State Conservation and Archaeology Rescue Project (SCRAP) brought another group of eleven apparently determined to best the others. They worked 10-hour days for a total of 880 hours. Dick, who knew well how his crew functioned, made one request before they came, however. "Is there a coffee pot at the camp?" he asked. "This could be critical." A good many in the camp were fueled by coffee, and working long days required gallons of the stuff.

Bruce Bradley, now professor of prehistory at Exeter University in England, brought several groups over the years. The Houston Museum of Natural Science sent a group of kids under the watchful eye of Pam Wheat Stranahan to participate in excavation and record-keeping. "It's important for kids to learn about science," said Pam. "Science is how we work through problems. The kids loved it when Mike joined them at lunch, then took a nap in a wheelbarrow!" One day, the kids stealthily laid a bouquet of wildflowers on Mike's chest as he slept draped across the conveyance. It would have been a shame to disturb him.

Many more individuals came on their own. "I always wanted to learn about the development of mankind," said Doris Howard, a Gault volunteer citizen scientist. "It's very interesting to think about what has changed about who we are and where we came from. It's fun. I get to learn about things that are so different, so exciting. The things that people left behind. These were real people."

It wasn't difficult to get volunteers, explained Clark Wernecke, now executive director of the Gault School of Archaeological Research (GSAR). Such volunteers are often "passionate about archaeology. It's an adventure,"

he said. "People like to say, 'Oh, I worked at such-and-such site one time'. It just sounds neat. And remember, we'd been on CNN, Nova, in *Smithsonian Magazine*, and others so a lot of people knew about us."

"[We] like to do unusual things," explained Doris. "We're not afraid to get hot and dirty and work hard. Plus, we're always laughing and carrying on."

This book tells about the people at Gault: the ancient ones, the modern ones, and the ones in between.

Mike Collins

It was early February 1991 when Mike Collins, a tall man with graying hair, looked at the pile of dirt. The bottom of the pile was sticky black clay, but the top was crumbly and yellow. His eyes darted from the hole to that top dirt and back again. He took two steps and picked up a rock from the top of the pile. He brushed it off, studying it intently.

"Here's one you forgot," he said finally. The others crowded in to see the faint lines as he turned the small rock over in his hands.

"Well I'll be a jack rabbit!" said David. "It sure is!"

David took it in his hands to look at the strange lines lightly engraved on the stone. Mike took a step to the left and then dropped down on his hands and knees. He brushed light-colored dirt away from another small stone and picked it up.

"Here's another one."

"I'll be durned! How did you see that? I swear I looked all through that dirt and never saw a thing," howled David.

"Aw, I've been looking at this stuff since I was twelve years old," Mike chuckled.

Mike Collins has always loved the soil of the earth. He loves the way it looks, the way it feels in his hands, the way it crumbles—or not—and the way it holds mysteries we are only beginning to understand. Mike has been directing the research at Gault for more than twenty-six years now. He started the Gault School of Archaeological Research in 2006 and established the Prehistory Research Project in 2010, first at the University of Texas at

◀ Working near the bottom of Area 15 where Clovis and older than Clovis materials were found.

Mike Collins's fascination with nature and the environment began at a young age. He is around twelve years old in this picture.

Austin and then at Texas State University in San Marcos, for the analysis and curation of Gault materials.

When Mike was a young teenager, he was taught to look at landscape critically and to think about what lay underneath by geologist Glen Evans. Evans had been assistant director of the Texas Memorial Museum in Austin, when he moved to Midland, Texas, in 1953 to work for an oil company. There were probably more geologists in Midland than any place in the world at that time. The Permian Basin oil field was booming. Through some acquaintance Evans met the young Mike, and they bonded instantly. The geologist took the young boy out to look at the oil fields and surrounding areas, and teach him about the mysteries of the land.

"One of the first times I went out in the sand dunes with him," Collins recounted, "he pointed out some concentric circles in the sand. 'Look, it's this little root,' he said. 'When the wind blows, it blows it around, leaving a little track.'"

Evans was interested in how the physical features of the earth's surface interacted with the deep geology below. He taught Mike how to observe the surface of the earth with an eye to what lies underneath. As Collins recalled, "He would say, 'See that hill over there? See how it looks different from that one over there? That's because of . . .'" Evans talked to young Mike about the landscape and explained how it changed.

"Evans was doing some geologic mapping in the Marathon basin one time. He was looking at some geologic beds, and he couldn't see the difference on the ground. He was getting pretty frustrated. He sat down as the sun was going down, and he saw in the dying light that the grass was different from one spot to another. Later he figured out which grasses grew on what kind of rock. He then determined that he could use the grass patterns to map the underground geology." A brilliant deduction all from a simple observation. "Those little lessons like that were beyond priceless," said Mike.

"The loud and clear message that Evans gave me is that the surface of the earth is way more dynamic than most people think. More than most archaeologists think. There is constant change. Geomorphic processes are going on all the time," said Collins.

"Even though I had a wonderful relationship with my natural father, Evans was my intellectual father. He taught me a great deal. Of the many intellects I've known, he was the most complete naturalist of them all." Evans had a rare talent for observing the natural world, and he also had a prodigious curiosity. Today Evans is known as one of the founders of geoarchaeology, a multidisciplinary approach that uses the techniques and knowledge of geology to inform archaeological research. Evans also studied ancient animal bones, using multiple sources of evidence to learn the secrets held by the ground itself.

This multidimensional approach has been advantageous for Mike through the years, but at first, his techniques were simple. In fact, the first tool he used in archaeology was his ever-present pocket knife. As a young teenager, he liked to ride his scooter out to the dry fields on the edge of Midland. One day he stopped the scooter at the end of a row and saw a piece of chert sticking out of the ground near the back tire. He got out his pocket knife and dug it out. Even though it was only a reworked nub, that was the first Clovis-style projectile point he ever discovered. A complete Clovis point is long and slender, and is considered by archaeologists as the chief indicator of a hunter-gatherer culture that prevailed for about six hundred years, thirteen thousand years ago in North America. Mike was likely the first person to hold that worn out point in his hand since an ancient hunter dropped it all those years ago.

Mike's father encouraged his interests by taking him to look for arrowheads as a boy in West Texas. The family traveled to Mesa Verde National Park and other sites in the Southwest on summer vacations, and the young boy was impressed with what he saw. Then when he was twelve years old, a human skull was uncovered by blowing sand on a ranch about ten miles south of town. This turned out to be a critical experience for Mike.

An oil company employee had been walking a gas pipeline through a ranch one day to check for leaks, as was common at the time. The man wandered down a slight draw and discovered the weathered skull, where the sand had blown away. He notified the Museum of New Mexico about his discovery. Fred Wendorf, a new research archaeologist at the museum, drove over from Santa Fe to dig a few holes and see what he could find. After some preliminary excavation, Wendorf called E. H. Sellards, one of the prominent scholars of early man at the time and director of the Texas Memorial Museum in Austin, to join him at the Midland site. Several others, including the young T. N. Campbell, later professor of anthropology at the University of Texas, also came to witness the excitement.

Evans wrangled an invitation for Mike to tag along on the excursion with Sellards, who happened to be Evans's old boss, and the other experts. Mike even attended the luncheon that followed and heard the scholars discuss what they had seen. Various other material had been found near the skull, including mammoth bone, a grinding stone, a hearth, and several Folsom spearpoints, which were around twelve thousand years old. After this event, Mike's mind was made up: he wanted to be an archaeologist.

As time went on, both Evans and Campbell continued to mentor Mike in his growth as a scientist of the past. Mike's father built him a glass-topped storage case to display his arrowheads and spearpoints. The lanky teenager carefully typed labels for each one using the new listing and categorization of these stone tools just published in 1954 by the Texas Archeological Society (TAS). He wasn't very interested in the ordinary things kids did in those days, but he became a lifetime member of TAS at age twelve. In 2011, he received the Lifetime Achievement Award from that organization.

Another discovery crystallized his interest a few years later, as if any more were needed. While on a family trip to visit friends on a ranch at Langtry,

Texas, on the Rio Grande, Mike took a bucket and a shovel and hiked down a little canyon about a mile long. He was going to Ice Box Cave, where people had noted large animal bones jutting out of the broken rocks at the bottom of the cliff for years, without thinking much about it. As Mike used his emerging archaeological skills to dig around some of the bones on the surface, he noticed that the bones were charred like they had been burned. Maybe they were cattle bones? But the land was too dry to raise cattle, and the rancher only had goats. Maybe they were buffalo? But if so, why were there so many of them, and why were they burned? The teenager had many questions.

Michael B. Collins in his work uniform. He has studied Clovis and earlier than Clovis artifacts from all over North and South America.

He lugged a huge jawbone back home for Evans to see. Evans identified the bone as the mandible of the American buffalo (*Bison bison*), and theorized the burning might have been connected to ancient people who were known to have lived in the canyon. Mike's discovery became known as Bonfire Shelter, the scene of several episodes of presumed buffalo jumps. Turns out the bones were more than two-thousand years old. A wonderful mural depicts a similar event in the Visitors' Center at Seminole Canyon State Park and Historical Site near Del Rio, Texas, and drawings are included in almost every textbook on Texas history.

With a childhood like this, it is not surprising that Collins studied archaeology at the University of Texas at Austin and then earned his PhD from the University of Arizona. After a stint teaching at the University of Kentucky, Mike returned to Texas to stay.

Some might say it was pure luck that Mike Collins was on the backdirt pile at Gault that day in 1991. Others might contend it was being in the right place at the right time with the right preparation. At any rate, it was fortunate that Mike knew his way around dirt. He had spent the previous twenty years investigating geoarchaeology in Honduras and Kentucky, stone technology in Texas and Chile, hunter-gather lifeways, and Clovis blades. He observed the land, and the stuff hidden beneath the surface with a keen eye. He'd had his hands in a lot of dirt.

In 1991 David Olmstead decided to have professional resin casts made of his "hot dog bun" stones, so he contacted a well-known lab to do the work. The craftsman who ran the casting lab had made many plastic casts of fragile artifacts for museums around the county, and had a good reputation. The two inscribed stones and the reworked point they surrounded were cast in resin, yielding realistic representations with only slight differences in color. The creamy white and pink chert of the blade just can't be matched by plastic. The lightly etched drawings on the rocks are clearly visible to the naked eye.

Later David sent the lab another stone he had found at the Gault farm. This one he called the "wheat stone" because the etching reminded him of stalks of wheat. When the craftsman saw the stones David had found, he urged David to call Thomas R. Hester, then director of the Texas Archeological Research Lab at the University of Texas in Austin, before doing anything else. David invited Hester to visit the Gault farm, which was then owned by the Lindsey family. They walked the stream to see the piles of dirt dug every which way along the banks after sixty-five years of amateur arrow-head hunting. Hester asked if he could bring a colleague to see the place the next day. That person was Mike Collins. Collins did an informal walking survey of the Gault farm, and knew by the way the land was situated—the geomorphology, if you will—that there were likely to be ancient artifacts still buried under the dirt.

Collins noted the following in his field journal for February 2, 1991: "Extensive area of extremely complex geology and archaeology. Area of 'paleomounds' is partially drowned with elevated water table. Took numerous photos. Found four engraved stones in backdirt where D.O. claims to have found such stones with Clovis. Work at this site to determine actual stratig[raphy] and to search for context of the engraved stones is of paramount importance."

Tom Hester's field journal entry for that day added a warning note for people who would work there in the future: "TICKS!!" (underlined twice in the original).

2 What Is Clovis?

The term "Clovis" refers to an archaeological culture with distinctive stone technology and artifact styles in the Americas dated between 12,900 and 13,500 years ago, a bit older than the end of the last retreating glaciers of the Ice Age. The name comes from the dust-blown town of Clovis, New Mexico. A young girl bestowed the name Clovis on the little train stop of Riley Switch in eastern New Mexico in 1906. She was a well-read girl, and chose the name Clovis after a fifth-century Frankish king by that name. This little community was the closest outpost of civilization to Blackwater Draw, where E. B. Howard found a fluted spearpoint, now known as a Clovis point, in 1937. This was the first point of its type ever identified. Ranch hands had found pieces of chipped stone in Blackwater Draw years before, but when machinery began dredging the draw for gravel in the early 1930s, large animal bones came up in the mix. A local collector took Howard to the draw to get his opinion. By that time, a scouring wind had uncovered a large bed of Ice Age animal bones.

The point was mixed in with the bones of an extinct mammoth, which roamed North America at the end of the last Ice Age. Because of that, archaeologists figured the chert point must be about the same age. Edgar Billings Howard came to New Mexico seeking mammoth specimens for the American Academy of Natural Science Museum in Philadelphia. He thought the Blackwater Draw site was promising for his museum mission and set to work. After several years of excavation, Howard uncovered the distinctive spearpoint of an Ice Age hunter jammed into the ribs of a felled mammoth. He also found other tools made of stone and bone that made up the hunter's tool kit.

The Clovis cultural period is distinguished by unique manufacturing techniques for stone spearpoints in particular. Clovis spearpoints have a certain lanceolate shape, like the leaves of walnut and butternut trees, somewhat oval and pointy at the tip. Distinctive, shallow grooves, called "flutes," extend from the base toward the tip of most Clovis points. These flutes may have aided ancient Americans in attaching the point to the end of a spear. Pristine Clovis points are typically three-to-five inches long or sometimes more, making them some of the largest projectile points in North America. About 85 percent were made of chert, or flint, like at Gault, although occasionally some were chipped from jasper, obsidian, or other stone. These characteristics distinguish a Clovis projectile point from spearpoints made in other time periods.

Bruce Bradley, one of the foremost experts in Clovis manufacturing technology in the world today, says that Clovis points have "a distinctive attitude of confidence, boldness, and flair." The points often show a degree of craftsmanship not found in many other cultural eras of stone toolmaking. "They exhibit traits that indicate they were more than a means of survival; they show that, at least in this aspect of Clovis life, they expressed an aesthetic and world view of confidence, 'art', and optimism. They also suggest levels of social development, such as focused teaching, not usually associated with early hunter-gatherers," says Bradley. Even to the untrained eye, Clovis points are sleek and beautiful.

Other than stone and a few bone tools, little remains of the people who lived during the Clovis age. Their life, their creativity is only partially revealed to us today. The only art or graphic symbols attributed to Clovis-era people are engraved stones, such as the ones David found. They did

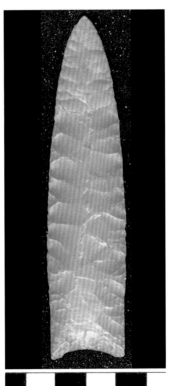

Classic Clovis projectile points, like this one from Blackwater Draw in New Mexico, were first identified around 1937.

not having writing, but they did have a concept of art, or representation of certain concepts that were no doubt meaningful to them. The people themselves lived in brush or hide shelters, or when the right place could be found, in overhangs in cliff walls called rockshelters. They did not have metal or pottery. We do not know what languages they spoke or what gods they worshipped. Even though the people probably wove baskets and matting, twisted string from plant fibers, and made clothing and other things out of leather and fur, we don't know much about these other crafts. The simple reason for this is that most organic materials, like basketry or animal hides, quickly deteriorate when left in nature (except in the driest of conditions). So the main clues we have about these ancient people are primarily made of stone. Distinctive stone tools like the Clovis point found at Blackwater Draw, specialized bone or ivory tools, and certain types of engraved stones, all found at Gault, are evidence of human workmanship and intellectual ability.

Clovis First Model

For a long time archaeologists and others assumed that the people who made Clovis points must have been the first human beings in America. This idea is known as the Clovis First Model (i.e., that the first people to arrive in the Western Hemisphere came during the Clovis cultural period about thirteen thousand years ago. This theory held sway for at least seventy years before evidence of earlier occupation began to be widely accepted by archaeologists.

The question of how human beings got to America in the first place intrigued many people for hundreds of years. As early as 1590, during a period of great oceanic exploration of the world, the Spanish priest Fray Jose de Acosta first suggested the idea that a land bridge had once existed between Asia and America. This notion gave rise to the theory that the earliest people to come to the American continents walked across the Bering Land Bridge following Pleistocene animals sometime toward the end of the last Ice Age. This theory was taught to American schoolchildren for many years, and most readers can probably visualize a map of the Bering Strait Land Bridge from their schoolbooks.

The people who arrived were thought to be big game hunters, who chased mammoths with a spear. In a span of five hundred years or so, according to this theory, most of the large game animals of the last Ice Age were hunted to extinction by what must have been a relatively small group of initial explorers. These were mighty hunters who brought down fourteen-foot-tall mammoths with only the strength of their spears. But now, after a great deal of further research, scholars are beginning to realize the Clovis First theory may not be correct. There is no doubt, however, that around thirteen thousand years ago, people physically and intellectually similar to us could be found living in most parts of what is now the United States.

Other Clovis Sites in Texas

People lived all around what is now the state of Texas during the Clovis period. At least 136 locations in Texas have yielded evidence of Late Paleoindian (10,000 years ago) to Clovis (13,500 years ago) occupation. For example, about 300 yards downstream from the Gault site on Buttermilk Creek, Mike Waters of Texas A&M University dug another area dubbed the Debra L. Friedkin site. Waters had worked at Gault in 2000. Not unexpectedly, he found Clovis-age tools at Friedkin. An analytic technique called optically stimulated luminescence (OSL), which determines dates from the soil itself instead of carbon, returned dates between 13,200 and 15,500 years before present. In addition, about 15,500 flakes and other artifacts were recovered from a layer of cultural deposition below the Clovis-age material found at the site. Thus the Buttermilk Creek Complex of workshops and living areas continued beyond the modern boundaries of the Gault site itself. Archaeologists often use information gained from one site to interpret another of approximately the same age, so an abundance of sites with similar traits leads to increased certainty of interpretation of evidence.

A rockshelter about 225 miles southwest of Gault on the Sabinal River preserved more evidence of Clovis life. Kincaid Shelter was originally excavated in 1948 by Mike's mentors, Glen Evans and E. L. Sellards from the Texas Memorial Museum. T. N. Campbell, whom Mike had also met in Midland as a young boy, conducted a university field school at the shelter in 1953 for UT Austin.

Engraved stones, much like the ones found at Gault, were found at Kincaid, suggesting similar lifestyles of the groups who lived at each place. A strange, purposeful array of river cobbles inside the shelter indicates that

What Is OSL?

Optically stimulated luminescence, or OSL, is a method of
dating sand or quartz grains in soil. Because the technique
uses the physics of ionizing radiation, the results are considered generally accurate but not precise. In other words, there
can be a fairly large margin of error. For example, a sample
might yield an OSL date of $12,300 \pm 900$ years. However,
depending on how exacting the methods are, multiple individual sand grains can be dated and the result averaged to
narrow the margin of error to a few hundred years. Events
that can be dated this way include the mineral's last exposure
to heat or sunlight. In other words, scientists can determine
when a sample of dirt taken from twelve feet underground,
for instance, last saw daylight. If the soil has not been disturbed, OSL techniques indicate when that bit
of dirt was last on top of the ground.

the people who lived there carried smoothed rocks from the river below to create some sort of flooring. The people at Kincaid ate turtles, frogs, fish, and maybe even an alligator or two from the nearby river. The people also had to contend with large Pleistocene animals that were there in Clovis times as well. For example, archaeologists found the tooth of the now extinct cave lion in the shelter. Perhaps that tooth was a talisman of some sort, or a hunting trophy, or both. At least it was not sunk into human bone!

Clovis-age people stopped temporarily near a spring in Yellowhouse Draw, located in the city of Lubbock, Texas, today, to hunt and butcher mammoths and other animals. The site was first excavated by the Works Progress Administration in 1939–41. Glen Evans, who only a few years later would begin to mentor a young boy named Mike, and E. H. Sellards carried out work there in the early 1950s. Today there is a wonderful museum with life-size bronze statues of Ice Age animals at a visitors' center.

The Alibates chert quarry archaeological area is about thirty-five miles north of Amarillo, Texas. The beautiful Alibates stone was highly prized by Clovis peoples and others, and has been found as far away as Idaho. The worn-out point David Olmstead found in between two engraved stones was made of Alibates chert. Some of the tools recovered from Blackwater Draw in New Mexico are also made of this material. The stone can be banded red or purple, with a creamy texture that is unmistakable. The National Park Service has built a very good museum and visitors' center there for people interested in learning more about this important mineral resource.

Two Late Paleoindian sites in Texas, dating back about eleven thousand years, are also instructive about ancient lifeways. About twenty miles outside of Austin near the suburb of Round Rock, Texas, is the Wilson-Leonard archaeological site. There beside a creek, a young woman was buried about eleven thousand years ago. She was placed in a flexed position with a worn grinding stone beside her. Originally excavated in the early 1980s, cultural deposits at Wilson-Leonard went down more than nineteen feet in the silty soil near the stream. This location contained buried artifacts from every time period known in Texas, from historic to Clovis and perhaps beyond.

Another human burial site, known as Horn Shelter, northwest of Waco, Texas, on the Brazos River lay undisturbed until the late 1960s, when avocational archaeologists excavated there. An adult and a juvenile were buried together around eleven thousand years ago, about the same time as Wilson-

Leonard, with the juvenile facing the adult's back. Both skeletons were facing west, and were in remarkably good condition. Many shell beads or ornaments were found around the grave, along with turtle shells that may have been used to hold pigment, like red ocher. The bodies were covered with slabs of stone, but not the heads. The people who lived in that shelter sometimes hunted buffalo, but depended on small animals for much of their food. Like Gault, this shelter is located in the juncture of the Blackland Prairie and Cross Timbers environmental regions, providing a mix of prairie and woodland habitats.

Clovis Colonization

Clovis-age material has been found not only in New Mexico and Texas, but also across other parts of what is now the United States, and into Mexico, Belize, Costa Rica, Panama, and the northernmost part of Venezuela. Concrete evidence of our human ancestors' time upon the earth, such as particular stone points, blades, and cores, has been found in many locations in these areas. Clovis artifacts have been found in most of the lower forty-eight states of the United States, although they are sparse in California and the Great Basin. Until recent decades, researchers generally agreed that the Clovis-age people were the first to inhabit the American continents.

Evidence of Clovis-era people has been found in at least 1,500 different places in the United States, from coast to coast, and south to Central America. For example, in 1913 ancient human bones were discovered near Vero Beach, Florida. E. H. Sellards, whom we'd met before, also recovered an engraved mammoth tusk, as well as various Clovis-age stone tools from this Florida spot. Today the human bones still do not have an exact date, but the fact that they were found in context with Pleistocene animals likely points to Clovis times. In the mid-1970s, also near the East Coast, more than 55,000 Clovis-age lithic, or stone, artifacts were recovered from the Shawnee-Minisink archaeological site about a hundred miles north of Philadelphia, Pennsylvania. Out west, the Murray Springs mammoth kill site in Arizona, excavated during the late 1960s, contained bones from mammoths, extinct bison, horses, camels, and wolves or dogs, along with stone projectile points, a bone tool, and several other lithic artifacts. In Costa Rica, several Clovis-like points were found in a plowed field in 1975. In the Sonoran Desert of

Mexico, the jaw of a Pleistocene gomphothere, a large elephant-like proboscidean, was discovered in 2007 along with several distinctive Clovis points, including two stunning examples made of clear quartz.

Clovis Stone Tool Technology

Clovis stone tool technology emerged sometime around 13,500 years ago in North America. No other place in the world at that time used exactly the same techniques for working stone. Clovis technology is one of the great American inventions, just like the light bulb or baseball. In fact, it may have been the first American invention.

Today we often use the term "technology" to mean electronic technology like computers and smartphones, practical things that are supposed to make our lives easier. But two hundred years ago, the word "technology" usually referred to the study of "useful arts," such as ship building or weaving cloth. The word itself just means the manner in which some practical object or effect is produced. This can include the techniques and materials for manufacturing widgets of some sort, as well as scientific knowledge that is applied for practical purposes, such as "space technology."

Clovis-era people used the science and technology of their time to understand the natural world and invent useful things to solve problems. The people applied what they learned to make useful tools for everyday life. Making high-quality stone tools required certain skills learned through observation and experimentation. Clovis stone tool technology involved chipping flakes off larger stones in a manner and pattern developed through experimentation and observation. Through trial and error, we assume, "Joe" Clovis, likely working together with his pals, discovered several special techniques for taking thin flakes off rough chert in order to make sharp spearpoints. Joe used the material he had, whether that be jasper, Alibates chert, obsidian, Edwards chert, quartz, or some other suitable stone that would hold a sharp edge. Some women and men became experts at making stone points or bifaces or other types of tools. Some were just learning. Most were in the middle. We should assume that everyone in the band or group knew the basics of how to make a stone tool. Just as they learned to make fire, perhaps with a fire drill or other device, children could easily imitate their elders, chipping a sharp flake off a larger stone to use for cutting. Women and men fashioned sharp bifaces to cut plants or animal flesh, projectile points, and numerous other implements.

Making tools from stone is a process of reduction, chipping off bits of certain sizes and shapes from a larger rock to form the desired finished product, like sculpting from marble. The different shapes and functions of stone tools have been classified by archaeologists, and are often diagnostic of particular periods in time.

The first necessity for making a sharp tool out of rock is to locate the right kind of stone. The stone must have the ability to hold a sharp edge and break in certain ways in order to be useable for making a tool or dart point. High quality grayish-blue chert is found in ledges, seams, nodules, and cobbles all around the Gault site. Chert breaks in a predictable fashion, according to the affable Clark Wernecke. In addition, it holds a sharp edge—perfect for making projectile points that will stave off a bear or feed the band.

At Gault, people used some of the best stone on the continent to make thousands and thousands of tools for their everyday lives. Almost all of the tools and tool fragments found at Gault are made of Edwards chert, which juts out of the bank of the creek and is easily found around the area. "Edwards chert is just simply very good. It is the largest formation of good stuff in North America. But there is also plenty of crappy Edwards," commented Sergio Ayala, lithic technologist with GSAR. The reworked point David found in the offering was one of the few stones that came from another area. David's stone came from Alibates chert quarry, the prehistoric quarry located near Amarillo. Such stone was carried or traded all over North America because of its lustrous coloration and strong physical qualities.

A typical Clovis tool kit could have been carried in a small leather bag, perhaps nestled inside a carrying basket or a netted bag on a person's back. Like any good tool kit today, the Clovis kit contained the essentials needed for doing a variety of work such as hunting, scraping hides, and making a new spearpoint if one broke off in the side of a giant sloth or some such.

The Spread of People and Technology

Around 13,500 years ago, someone, maybe an early-day Steve Jobs, or a couple of people, like Jobs and Wozniak, had a "brilliant manufacturing idea," according to Tom Williams, lithic analyst with GSAR. Tom is a tall, red-headed Brit who studied with Bruce Bradley. He describes this revolutionary idea as "sort of like the iPhone. [Apple] not only created a new technology but also the idea of the smart phone itself. What Clovis-age people did, like Apple, was to create a technology that brought together various technological elements in a way that was revolutionary. Just like there were other processors, touch-screens, telephones, etc, that worked as well as an iPhone, there were other types of stone tools that worked just as well as Clovis style ones, but iPhone and Clovis put the technologies together in a more useful way. Clovis manufacturing is more about *how* the projectile points were made than it is the shape of the point itself.

This amazing new technology spread so rapidly across the North American continent that "it's almost like a traveling salesman walked across the continent with his sample kit, showing people along the way this cool new thing," says Williams. People living in the Clovis period in North America used more or less the same techniques to make stone tools wherever they lived. In other words, a Clovis point found in New Mexico looks very much like a Clovis point found in Pennsylvania because they were made the same way. Bruce Bradley notes subtle differences, however, saying, "There is a wide range of approaches with some regional and possibly chronological variations. However, they are more alike than different and all express the distinctiveness of the period."

"There may have been regional dispersions of technical knowledge," according to Ayala. "Maybe it was an idea moving across social groups. Technological information is vital [for us] not only to understand their manufacturing processes, but it also allows us as archaeologists to map out social groups and how technology moves through them."

Apparently people liked what they saw and quickly adopted this new way of doing things. Both the concept and the technology spread across North America in less than five hundred years—and that's without social media! The big question is whether the people who had this brilliant idea were the same ones who populated the entire continent (remember they were walking and going about daily life the whole way, from coast to coast), or perhaps the traveling salesman found others already living in new places with whom to share his knowledge.

Mike Collins is somewhat troubled by the rapid technological expansion during Clovis times. He is wearing his standard uniform of long-sleeved button-up shirt in white, tan, blue, or green, with suspenders holding up his jeans or khakis as we talk. "It seems improbable," he says, "that one group of people could have adapted to all the various environmental habitats in North America in such a brief interval." He also wonders how different groups of people, if there were such groups living in North America at that time, could have adopted Clovis technology with so few changes to the basic pattern. In other words, how did population expansion and the spread of Clovis stone tool production happen so fast? Given the complexity of geography and environments in North America, these questions are real puzzles. They are some of the biggest questions with which archaeologists are currently wrestling as they attempt to understand the peopling of the Americas.

Most of the people who lived in the Americas thirteen thousand years ago are now identified with the name of an obscure town in eastern New Mexico—that is, Clovis. The primary way we know them is through the stone artifacts they left behind. Besides incised stones of unknown purpose, they made specially fluted projectile points; long, sharp-edged flakes called *prismatic blades*; several forms of retouched blades; and flakes and lithic production debris, called *debitage*, all found at Gault. Stone workers at Gault learned the exact way to hit the stone from an elder or teacher, or a traveling salesman, but mostly by practicing the craft. Sometimes the stone would break the wrong way due to an imperfection in the stone itself. Sometimes it would break due to the inexperience of the worker. And sometimes the tool would be ruined simply by accident, a slight miscalculation of force or angle. Any place chert has been worked like this for any amount of time will accumulate considerable debris. Clovis-era people left a trail of chert flakes as they migrated to almost every part of the United States and other places, including a little stream in Central Texas.

3 Evidence of Clovis Life

Mike knew there would be plenty of evidence indicating ancient human activity at the Gault site when he found another engraved stone on David's backdirt pile in 1991. But not only did Mike's crew eventually unearth an extensive stone tool manufacturing center at Gault; they also discovered several other indications of Clovis culture that present a more diverse picture of life in that long-ago time. Gault turned out to be a very rich site for artifacts, especially for Clovis. Other major evidence of Clovis life found at Gault includes a few remains of Ice Age animals, a bone tool, and intricately carved stones. These differing lines of evidence add more pixels to our picture of daily life among Clovis-era people.

The Stone Tool Workshop

Sergio Ayala sat on a bucket one afternoon in the GSAR lab at Texas State University, demonstrating how to chip flakes off a chunk of chert. "For me, flintknapping was a lot of trial and error at first. I was trying to make different tools and use different techniques. Over a period of time I started to narrow the possibilities and know what was likely." Chink. A flake fell on the concrete floor.

Sergio primarily studies stone working from the Archaic period, or roughly from ten thousand to about two thousand years ago in North America. In addition to more than six hundred thousand chert flakes from the Clovis period found at Gault, a huge number of "younger" bits from the Archaic

13,110 Years Ago

Tocho was sitting in the shade by a quiet stream, carefully chipping flakes of gray stone off a cobblestone core in his hand. He turned the core over and looked up. The stone was about the size of two hands pressed together when he started, but it was trimming up nicely. He studied the smooth surface scar where the last flake had been knocked off and rubbed it with his thumb. He lightly tossed the hammerstone in his right hand. Then, clink, he knocked off another piece.

It clattered to the ground, which was covered with shards of chert. He had been working half the day, mostly to keep his mind off Sibu, but also because the band needed fresh, sharp tools. Many of the old ones were worn to nubs. He turned the half-worked core over, back and forth, studying the structure of the breaks he was creating. He had to figure out the best spot to strike the hammer next, so the core didn't accidentally split. So far no flaws had been uncovered in the stone—it looked good.

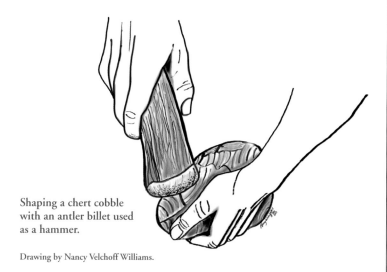

Shaping a chert cobble with an antler billet used as a hammer.

Drawing by Nancy Velchoff Williams.

Even today, visitors walking around Gault find chert flakes scattered on the surface. Gault was the site of a stone tool manufacturing center thousands of years ago.

He put down the hammer and ran his free hand over the face of the rock. This was an art done by touch and feel, more than anything. He liked what he felt. One or two more strikes and the core would be exhausted. Then he would choose a piece that had been struck off to finish as a nice spearpoint. That's the part he liked best—using an antler tine to take off fine, little flakes along the edges. He rearranged the leather apron on his knee and took up the hammerstone again.

Tink! Another blade landed at his feet. He raised his hammer for the final blow, when Payat came running.

"Tocho! Come! Come now!" cried the boy, just as Tocho swung his arm.

The hammer landed crudely on the core and split it across the middle. Tocho stood up quickly as the ruined stone fell to the ground.

"The baby's coming," blurted Payat. "Come now!"

period were recovered in the upper levels of excavation. Sergio's task was to recreate these Archaic flakes in order to study the process of manufacture.

"I was trying to get large spalls," he said, "taking macroflakes off a large piece of chert, a bit larger than a football. Trying to remove long straight flakes. That is the basis for a projectile point." He turned the core on his knee and looked at it, sizing it up for the next blow. Like any flintknapper, he used a hammerstone for this part of the process. Later he would use an antler billet, or short club-like tool, to finish shaping the piece.

"Patterns in flakes showed me a technological behavior that we could quantify. The way flakes were releasing off bifaces gave me an idea of the technology. It opened up the tool kit [of the people] and their behavior to me."

Sergio is one of a few twenty-first century archaeologists re-learning how to use methods and materials from thousands of years ago in order to replicate Archaic and older Clovis technology. In the 1960s, few people in the United States or the rest of the world knew how to make stone tools of any kind, much less Clovis points. Don Crabtree was a pioneer in experimental flintknapping, and basically learned from his mistakes how to flake stone effectively. He spent more than thirty years assisting and teaching others to recreate ancient stone tools, and consulted at Blackwater Draw with E. B. Howard and at the Smithsonian Institution until his retirement in 1975. His 1972 book *Introduction to Flintworking* is still required reading for those who wish to master the craft.

When Bruce Bradley was in high school, he saw a brief flintknapping demonstration by Crabtree. After years of experimenting on his own, Bradley eventually studied with Crabtree and Françoise Bordes, then professor of prehistory at the University of Bordeaux, France, and others. Bradley had been inspired to make stone tools as a child when he saw a collection of Indian relics. On a family trip he bought a chunk of obsidian and "proceeded to smash it to bits" for lack of any information on how to turn stone into knives and other useful things. That started him on a long process through which he learned the basics.

Bradley is coprincipal investigator for the Gault School of Archaeological Research. After experimenting for many years to reproduce stone-age tool technology, he is now considered one of the world's experts in this field. He has brought groups of volunteers to work at Gault several times,

Bruce Bradley demonstrates the ancient art of flintknapping using a large antler billet.

often spending delightful evenings around the campfire flintknapping with his colleagues. "Today's work at Gault was nearly ideal," he wrote in March 2000. There is even a video of him making stone tools under a tree at Gault, just as Tocho might have done.

"Sergio likens flintknapping to chess, thinking several steps ahead," said Jennifer Gandy, a precise, quiet young woman who also works for GSAR. She spends most of her time intensely studying chert flakes about the size of a fingernail. To see Jennifer in the lab is to see a woman bent over trays and trays of gray chert flakes, scrutinizing them under a microscope from time to time, recording the differences and likenesses she sees in each one. Her detailed comparative work is helping to build a better understanding of how stone tools were made, flake by flake, and how prehistoric people utilized the resources in their environment.

"I was always interested in rocks, fossils, and arrowheads," she said. "I've always liked organizing, sorting, categorizing, compartmentalizing. I find it very calming. There is always something to learn even in things you've looked at before. That's part of the fun."

"Flintknapping is sort of like getting the statue out of the marble," she continued. "We have trouble making the stuff ancient people made. We have a lot of experimental archaeology going on to try to learn the thought processes of the people as well. There are a series of decisions with each hit. Connecting the dots takes a lot of experience looking at flakes and thinking about it." Jennifer carefully spread out the next batch of chert chips she was going to examine on the table. She adjusted her microscope so she could see exactly how each flake had been struck. "You can learn just as much if not more from flakes," she added, "about how humans think and make tools as you can from an arrowpoint or other tools. Now it is obvious to me, but not when I first started. It takes a different perspective to really see it."

Robert Lassen sauntered over to observe Sergio and join the conversation. "The physics of the stones is pretty well-known," he explained as another chip fell to the floor. "[Chert breaks with a] conchoidal fracture, like glass. Controlling how the stone breaks is what flintknapping is all about."

In addition to millions of chert flakes, at least forty complete, or nearly so, Clovis projectile points have been found at Gault over the years by both volunteers and professional archaeologists. The compelling evidence of the broken chert itself allows archaeologists to state with confidence that the area around Buttermilk Creek was indeed a stone tool manufacturing site thousands of years ago. Many of these bits were found in their original place, or in situ, which means that the artifact was found where it dropped on the ground and had no evidence of being moved there by environmental means. This is significant because the placement gives credible context to the discovery. Points are generally recorded in field journals and usually cause a bit of excitement when found. But flakes, on the other hand, were sometimes carried out of Gault by the bucketful.

May Hamilton Schmidt remembered when another volunteer found an almost complete Clovis point made of quartz. "Even with dirt on it, it was so clear you could read field notes through it," she recalled. Quartz does not occur naturally at Gault or anywhere nearby, so it must have been carried in from somewhere else. Sharon Dornheim, who worked at Gault as a graduate student, remembers that someone else found a "gorgeous Clovis blade" at Gault. "It was perfect," she said, "like a textbook photograph."

Mike found a Clovis point in situ once, in the wall of a trench his crew was digging. Bruce Bradley was there at the time and helped Mike expose it. They worked with the tip of a trowel and a bamboo skewer so as not to accidentally obscure any faint use-wear evidence.

On another day Bruce noted "a magnificent conical blade core" that had just been unearthed. "It is clearly Clovis, but out of primary content," or not in situ, he went on. When an artifact is out of primary context, that means more work for archaeologists to figure out where in time and space the artifact actually belongs.

Another conical blade core was documented in situ by Mike. "This is a significant addition to the diagnostic Clovis assemblage," he concluded. Stan Ahler, then with Northern Arizona University, brought volunteer groups to Gault several times. He wrote in his journal for March 10–24, 2001, that they were enduring several days of cold, soggy weather, but finding "Clovis preforms, blades, and flakes." He declared March 22 was "a very bifacial day . . . a Clovis carpet."

More than 50 percent of all stone tool manufacture resulted in failure, estimates Andy Hemmings in the book *Clovis Technology*. In other words, more than half of the bifaces that people attempted to make broke and had to be discarded, thus creating the "Clovis carpet." This, plus all the thinning flakes and sharpening flakes produced in a work session, resulted in enormous debitage, or chert flake debris, at Gault, and helped archaeologists identify the place unequivocally as a stone tool workshop.

"Mike asked for lab volunteers so I responded to the call," explained Jonelle Miller-Chapman, a citizen scientist who worked on the Gault project for about ten years off and on.

"We worked on sorting tiny debitage into groups by size. Later I was one of a few others who processed artifacts recovered from a TAMU summer school excavation at Gault. That lasted several years." Besides blades, cores, and debitage, other types of stone artifacts that clarify and enlarge current ideas about Clovis lifeways were also found at Gault. Examples include scrapers, or palm-sized stones sharpened only on one face. Scrapers could be hafted onto handles or simply held in the hand. They were commonly used for scraping connecting tissues and other goo off animal hides before tanning. People depended on animal hide for clothing, bed covers, rain tarps, and so on. It is likely that women, men, and children all made and used scrapers for various activities.

Two tools recently identified at Gault are the only examples of their types known from Clovis times. These two small stone tools have expanded the types of tools thought to have been used during the Clovis period. A slender

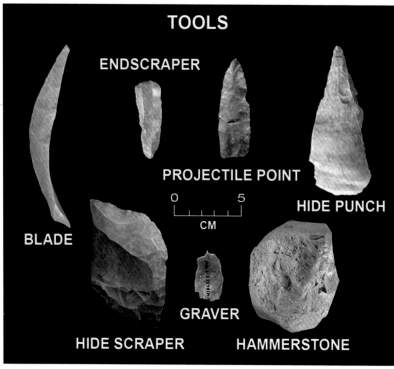

TOOLS

ENDSCRAPER

PROJECTILE POINT

HIDE PUNCH

0   5

CM

BLADE

HIDE SCRAPER

GRAVER

HAMMERSTONE

Some of the different varieties of stone tools recovered from Gault. Tools of bone and wood were also used by human beings before the discovery of metal.

prismatic blade, about seven centimeters long and two centimeters wide, with a tiny sharp beak on one end was identified as a graver. Often the small, sharp tip breaks off, and archaeologists don't recognize the stone's true function. This special stone was used like a jeweler's engraving tool, perhaps to chisel designs on other stones, like the incised stones found at Gault, for example, or other materials, such as wood or bone. "It might have been used for scarification," Mike conjectured. The slender blade was "an unusually fine [delicate] item for Clovis," he said. There is no direct evidence that people at Gault scarred or tattooed their skin, but it is not unlikely either.

An adze, a blunt-tipped tool similar to an ax and used for cutting or shaping wood, was also discovered at Gault "deep in a rocky layer at the base of a Clovis component," Collins recounted. "[This was] a first for Clovis, so far as I know," he continued. The tool is about 6 centimeters long by about 4.5

centimeters wide. Both the graver and the adze are remarkable not only for being the only objects of their kind identified so far from the Clovis period, but also because modern versions of these tools are still used today with very little change in basic design.

Researchers use a variety of methods to learn about the stone tool technology of Clovis-era peoples. Not only have some researchers experimented with techniques for reproducing stone tools; others have conducted use-wear analysis to determine exactly what the tools were used for. Marilyn Shoberg has identified certain Clovis tools found at Gault that were used for cutting grass or butchering meat, for example. She examined several stone tools under high magnification of 50× to 500× and photographed potentially diagnostic wear patterns with a digital microscope camera. When a stone tool is used, edges are modified by abrasion and minuscule flaking. Surface polishing and the orientation of striations characteristic of various materials present telling clues as to how the tool was used.

Marilyn Shoberg analyzing the use-wear, or micro-wear, found on artifacts to determine how tools were used. The analysis of artifacts takes years to reconstruct the technology and lifeways of ancient people.

Archaeobotanist Linda Perry from George Washington University examined the edges of thirty-five sample flakes and tools from Gault for microscopic remains of starch grains that come from plants. Archaeobotany is the study of ancient plant remains, which give clues to diet, season, climate, and other important factors of the human and natural environment. Sixteen of the samples yielded starch remains from various grasses, such as little barley and wild rye. Some of the samples had clearly been heated thousands of years ago, perhaps by boiling or parching. None had been ground into flour. This indicates that whole or cracked wild grass seeds were cooked by people at Gault, perhaps as some kind of porridge.

"The whole thing was awesome!" said James Beers. James was at Gault in 2002 and 2003 during some of the use-wear experiments. "I remember that on the night we arrived at Dr. Collin's property near Gault he showed us two large Clovis-age blades excavated from the site. Just seeing those and handling them for those few minutes pumped me up for the dig. Every day I couldn't wait to get up and start digging again."

Use-Wear Analysis

Use-wear analysis is a method of determining the function
for certain stone tools by examining the edges and surfaces
of a stone under a microscope to see characteristic patterns
of wear. For example, polish and minute striations on a stone
tool from cutting grass look different from those made by
cutting meat. Modern experimenters replicate an activity,
such as butchering a bison, using a stone tool similar to the
specimen they want to study. By comparing the marks on
the experimental tool with those on the archaeological tool,
researchers can infer if the two tools were likely used for the
same purpose.

Starch Grain Analysis

Starch grains, which are ubiquitous in plants, often remain in soil or on artifacts after all other plant remains have decayed. For example, a stone knife that was used to harvest plants may have grains of starch still adhering to the edge. The sample is observed using a compound microscope at high magnifications, and digital images are recorded. Analysts can learn which types of plants were growing in a particular place at a certain time and, in some cases, whether the starch grain was damaged or broken down by heating or cooking. This is helpful when trying to ascertain the diet of long-ago peoples as well as the environment.

13,500 years ago

They heard the beast trumpeting before they could actually see her. Two men dodged through the underbrush along the creek and scrambled up the shallow ridge. They crept through the dry summer grasses so the wind would not give them away. The huge animal bellowed again and the men flinched. Silently they watched.

The mammoth was at least twice as tall as the men at the shoulder. Her curved tusks, which were longer than a man, were dangerous weapons. She threw her head back and flung her trunk in the air, bringing down branches from huge overhanging trees. The animal struggled to pull a giant foot out of the deep muck that surrounded her. She strained to get a foothold on solid ground, but each time, the foot slipped before she could heave up her enormous body. She was getting tired.

Soon, thought the men. They backed off to the trees and ran down to the creek bed far enough away that the mired animal could not see nor smell them. They were willing to wait. No one but a fool would attack a giant mammoth with only an atlatl and a dart. Better to wait until the beast is exhausted and then ease her journey.

The Mammoth Mandible

In spring 1998, Howard Lindsey pushed the lever forward as the Bobcat scooped up another mouthful of dirt. He wrenched the machine into reverse and then jerked it forward to dump the tan soil onto the screen Ricky had set up over two sawhorses.

"Dad, Dad," Ricky waved his arms and yelled. "Stop a minute. Look at that!" Ricky pointed to the scrape in the dirt the Bobcat had just made. Howard cut the motor and jumped out.

"What is it?" asked Ricky.

"I don't rightly know," responded Howard. "Hand me a stick."

Ricky picked up a stick and gave it to his father. Howard Lindsey gently scratched the brownish dirt off what appeared to be a large animal bone.

"Too big for a cow," he said.

"Maybe it's a buffalo," guessed Ricky.

"Maybe." Howard scraped around the outline of the bone. "Go get one of your mother's garden tools," he commanded. "I'm gonna dig around in this and see what I can find."

Later that night around the kitchen table, Howard's wife suggested they call somebody who knew more about these things. "Better call Bryan," she said.

Bryan Jameson happened to be a long-time member of the Texas Archeological Society, and a well-respected avocational archeologist. He suggested the Lindseys, the owners of the Gault site property at that time, once again call in Tom Hester from UT Austin and his colleague Mike Collins. Tom and Mike had visited the site in 1991, after David Olmstead found the engraved stones with the worn-out point between them. After only a few weeks of testing in 1991 in areas likely to contain Clovis material in Mike's estimation, professional archaeologists had not been allowed back to the property.

The mammoth mandible lies upside down in the mud as it was found by the Lindseys. Removing the fragile jawbone from the ground was delicate, messy work.

The pay-to-dig operation continued, however, so there were even more shallow potholes all over the place. By 1998 the property had changed hands and Howard, the new owner, was more receptive to experts coming in to assess the buried stones and other material on their land.

Mike and others from the University of Texas at Austin arrived just about sun up on August 1, 1998, to take a look at the bones. Mike was excited to see them because they could offer another line of evidence for the engraved stones and Clovis points he had found seven years before. "ELL and Susan Hardin will jacket the exposed bone," Mike wrote in his journal. Ernie L. Lundelius is Professor Emeritus of Vertebrate Paleontology at UT Austin, and a well-known expert on Ice Age animals. For student Susan Hardin, it was her first day in the field. What a day it would turn out to be.

"Very hectic beginning," Mike continued in his journal. Howard and Ricky were milling around as Lundelius got down on his hands and knees. "Milton is photographing the diverse materials—many blade-like flakes, bifaces, etc. Ricky and Max found a Clovis point in loose dirt in floor of the pit . . . also a burin spall. . . . We found an unfinished Clovis point just beneath the bone concentration and large flake (biface, overshot). A bifacial preform was found in the . . . profile. It has Clovis-type work with a beveled base—maybe a preform. . . . The large flake and Clovis point are from top of gravel, just below the bone."

Of three areas of bone uncovered by Howard Lindsey, one turned out to be a mammoth mandible, or jaw, with the teeth facing down. It was under the water table in the gravel due to nearby springs. "The bone itself was so cracked we knew it would fall apart," said Mike, "very poor bone preservation." Getting any bone out was a slow, muddy process. As Lundelius was excavating around an ulna, or leg bone, he hit a stone tool laying next to it, which was the first time in his long career that he had ever found a tool in association with a Pleisticene bone. In his many years in the field, he was always after bone, not stone. This was a thrilling first for him. Then his student Susan, with beginner's luck on her side, uncovered a Clovis point on her first day ever in the field. Lundelius looked at her and chided in mock exasperation, "It's all downhill from here, my friend." Susan chuckled at her mentor's comment. It was a "pretty good day for discovery," added Mike.

On August 16, 1998, the crew arrived at 7:00 a.m. They had to work as much as possible in the morning before the heat sapped their energy and drained their ambition. They had done a lot the day before. "Excavation has been much enlarged and much of the deeper part is underwater," wrote Mike. "They also found many more blades, at least five more blade cores, a Clovis point, many preforms and preform fragments, and nearly a whole mammoth dental plate, plus many small fragments of large animal bones (including a bison), and much misc. [*sic*] worked chert." They continued taking out pieces of bone and stone artifacts for several days, all duly bagged and tagged by exact location. By September 5, the heat was intense. Mike wrote that they "began today by setting up sunshades [over the excavation units]. The priority today is to expose and jacket the mandible." But that statement was entirely too optimistic. Too many other things presented themselves that had to be done first.

Finally October 12 arrived. The mandible was still in the ground, wet and crumbly. Lundelius was going to make a plaster cast of the jawbone to remove it from the ground in one piece, but Mike was afraid the plaster wouldn't dry in time. If they had to leave it over night, water from the upwelling spring would cover it again and make the plaster useless. So he draped plastic kitchen wrap over the bone to form a moisture barrier. Lundelius had never seen anyone do that before, but concluded it was worth a try. Lundelius poured hardening chemicals over the bone, and then put on a layer of burlap and a layer of plaster.

"With all the wetness and the poor condition of the bone we may fail to get the plaster cast hard enough to successfully extract the specimen—we can't leave it overnight because spring flow will totally inundate the cast," wrote Mike that afternoon. It was a race against time and rising water.

The plaster didn't set until nearly dark. As they waited, Lundelius regaled them with stories of bone extractions he had worked on that crumbled into nothing when they were taken out of the ground. Everyone was a bit nervous.

At last Lundelius rapped his knuckles on the plaster shell and declared it ready to go. Carefully, carefully, the thirteen-thousand-year-old jawbone was lifted out of the ground. It had been a twelve-hour day and several months of work to get this far.

"It was amazing to see the mandible that day," commented Tamara Walter of Texas Tech University, who was working at the site at that time. "There was such a contrast between racing against the clock to save the site and

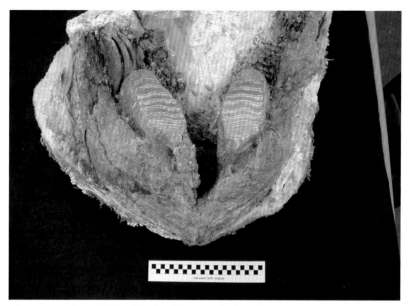

The mammoth mandible after the plaster cast had hardened shows out-of-place in-coming molars on either side of the large, wavy-looking grinding plates in the mouth of the young animal.

recover the information, and a sense of urgency to get as much information as possible. You could just tell that everyone was thrilled to be there."

The jaw was from an adolescent female mammoth. There were at least twenty-one artifacts associated with the mammoth. All of the artifacts were within a meter of the jawbone, including a Clovis point, a biface fragment, seven cores and core fragments, six blades, and some flakes. None of the artifacts or the mandible itself showed any signs of water tumbling or smoothing, so were likely to be in situ. Around the hole were an "unbelievable array of Clovis-age artifacts and fauna," or animal remains, according to Mike. Bone fragments, tusk fragments, a dental plate, and other materials were recovered. There could be more Ice Age animal bones to the east of the excavation pit according to Collins, but they didn't have the time, money, or opportunity to excavate that area.

We do not know exactly how the animal died. There was "nothing coherent about the artifacts," said Mike Collins. "Not a kill site in the usual sense.

Not enough bones around there for them to have killed it at that spot." Clark Wernecke disagrees, however. "Given the projectile point, the large number of butchering tools surrounding it, and the lack of any damage or water-rounding, the mammoth likely was killed and butchered right there near the spring. However, we do not have any signs of butchering since we don't have bone preservation of the proper bits (such as a leg bone), and unless the point is stuck in a bone, I can't prove the animal was killed by man either. I can tell you it did not die of old age, however, because the bones are those of an adolescent."

Today the huge bone is at the Gault School of Archaeological Research on the campus of Texas State University, still mostly in its plaster cast. The plastic wrap is clearly visible, shredded at the edges. The plaster and burlap are still mostly intact. Researchers once tried to extract the bone from the cast with power tools, but did not get far, as the burlap shredded and dulled the saw blades they had on hand. Lundelius's form was meant to last. White plaster still covers the brownish-tan bone. There are two large teeth on either side of the jaw, and two more malformed ones behind those. The mandible barely fits in the curation drawer, about two feet long, but it is safely pre-

Columbian mammoths could be ten to fourteen feet tall at the shoulder and have tusks up to nine feet long. Remains of these huge animals have been found in many parts of North America. Drawing by Nancy Velchoff Williams.

served for future study, whenever new technology may allow us to discover more about the life and times of this young mammoth.

Columbian Mammoths used to roam all over Central Texas 13,500 years ago. Mammoth bones have been found in most parts of the state. They ranged over the southern half of North America all the way to Costa Rica. Farmers plowing fields, stone companies mining gravel, highway construction crews, and others regularly reveal a jawbone here or a tusk there. In Waco, Texas, fossils from twenty-four mammoths can be seen lying as they died at Waco Mammoth National Monument, about seventy miles northeast of the Gault site. Erin Keenan Early, a zooarchaeologist working with the Gault materials, describes the Waco mammoths as "an excellent snapshot of a specific event." Those twenty-four mammoths died in a flood, apparently, with adults trying to lift infants to higher ground. They, along with their cousins the Wooly Mammoths and Jefferson's Mammoth, wandered over much of North America for perhaps fifty thousand years until the end of the last Ice Age when they became extinct.

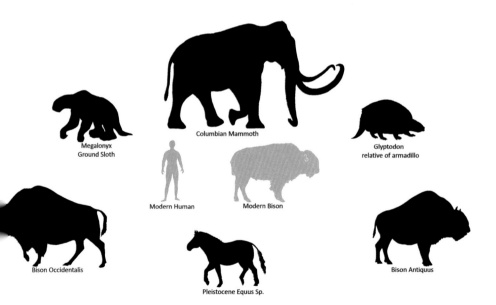

Human beings had to use their wits to hunt Pleistocene animals. Instead of always going for big game, however, they often ate rodents or turtles that were easier to catch. Drawing by Nancy Vechoff Williams.

Adult mammoths were built similar to a modern elephant, except for having greater size and a blackish, shaggy coat. They could be nine to fourteen feet tall at the shoulder, and weigh six to ten tons, or about twenty thousand pounds. Their tusks were often five to nine feet long. Their teeth had special ridges that helped them eat as much as four hundred pounds of leaves and bushes every day. In addition, they had long life-spans, perhaps fifty to eighty years for those who made it through adulthood.

Other Pleistocene animals also became extinct around thirteen thousand years ago, including saber-tooth cats, giant sloths, short-faced bears, dire wolves, two species of bison, and the giant armadillo-like Glyptotherium, among others. There are various theories about why this extinction may have occurred, including intense hunting (as in the Clovis First model), climatic change, disease, or most likely some combination of these events.

Bones from several other animals besides mammoths were also found at Gault over the years of excavation. Brigham Young University students noted finding bits of bison tooth and bone from one of the units they dug in summer 2000. Mike Collins jotted in his field journal about "uncovering pieces of bone" in October that same year. Jon Lohse, a graduate student at UT Austin in 2001, documented a big bone of some sort from one of the units, saying, "They exposed a very large bone protruding from the SW corner of the unit that may be a horse or bison." In August 2001 Howard Lindsey was running a Bobcat removing backdirt piles. A section of bone approximately about seven centimeters long and two centimeters wide, was recovered from the backhoe bucket. Dick Boisvert noted bone clusters and flake clusters in one of the New Hampshire units in April 2002. On February 13, 2010, Mike wrote that "a flat piece of very thin bone, perhaps a deer scapula, was found. It was only about three centimeters by two, and badly fragmented. This bone has a cross-hatch design carved into the exposed face. The bone will require removal in plaster." Something like this engraved bone will likely be studied for years as new researchers and technologies come along. Ashley Lemke, now at the University of Texas at Arlington, worked at Gault in January 2014 as part of her study of ancient humans in the Americas. In her field journal, she noted "many bone frags [sic] toward midden end of level 12—most very small, but bigger than a quarter." Then she added, "All will be mapped." These clues were carefully recorded, mapped, and labeled, and taken to the lab for further analysis.

According to Erin, the zooarchaeologist, the bone material she got from Gault "was a mess. A complete mess." Her job was to identify the animals represented by the bones that remained. But the bone fragments she had to work with were quite small, many only a quarter of an inch long. Some were powdery or chalky, and some were broken in such a way that the identifying features were no longer there. Most were heavily mineralized—far from ideal conditions for identifying ancient animals.

Collins says that "most faunal, or animal, bones in Central Texas cannot be identified beyond small, medium, or large because bone preservation is awful. We do have a few thousand pieces [from Gault], however, such as mammoth, horse, extinct bison, camel, modern bison, deer, canids, wolves or coyotes," for example.

Some bison and horse could be identified. Bison were identified from teeth. There were also a lot of deer-sized fragments, but Erin reserves final judgment on most of those. "To get any better identification," she says, pushing her hair to the side, "we would have to be very lucky."

Erin is using a new technology to study the Gault bones. Zooarchaeology by Mass Spectrometry, or ZooMS, relies on collagen in the organic material being studied. She is currently a graduate student at the University of Texas at Austin and working with groups at the University of York in England and the University of Copenhagen in Denmark, "because no place is doing this right now in the US, to my knowledge."

She explains:

> The process was developed in England, and it's similar to a genetic database. The more data we get, the more identifications we can make. Even after preparing the sample, the collagen protein is still too large to put in a mass spectrometer, so we have to break it up using an enzyme. This results in tiny fragments called *peptides*. We put tiny spots of solution containing these peptides on a metal plate, and put it in the mass spectrometer. The mass spectrometer, which looks like a box, about 2 feet by 1.5 feet wide, is equipped with an internal laser and connected to a computer. We point and shoot on the computer to fire the laser, which sends the peptides flying. The time from point A to point B in the mass spectrometer results in a spectrum, or signal, that I can read. I look at the peaks and try to match them to the database of previously

What Is ZooMS?

ZooMS is short for *zooarchaeology by mass spectrometry*, a system for analyzing animal collagen pioneered recently in England. Using tiny specimens of bone, ivory, teeth, antler, or skin, including leather and parchment, scientists can determine what type of animal the sample came from. For example, from a small bone fragment, scientists using ZooMS can determine whether the animal was a sheep or a goat. Because collagen is much more stable than ancient DNA, this technology can be used on extremely old materials, including those more than a million years old in some cases.

sequenced species. The more matches the better, but some species require a couple of hits and some just one.

To understand human behavior, "it's important to know how we interact with animals on a daily basis, and how important that is to a culture," Erin explains. "How it can define a culture . . . things that we do eat or don't eat; animals that we consider good pets or bad pets or social status pets; animals that we consider pests; whether we put out bird feeders; whether we wear feathers or wool or leather." By studying bone fragments, Erin hopes to learn more about the ancient people of Gault. For example, she suspects the people were at least in part eating small animals. "There is a lot of rabbit, turtle, wood rat, and microvertebrates" in the bone material, she explains. Discoveries like this are changing the old view that Clovis-age people were primarily mammoth hunters. Turns out they were primarily sustained by a mixed grill of terrapin, hare, and rodent.

A Strange Bone Tool

In February 2001, the blue and gold flag of New Hampshire fluttered now and then over the archaeological unit fondly called the "Hamster Pit" as the scrappy volunteers bent their trowels in the hard clay. Across the way, a maroon and white flag marked Texas A&M territory. It had been unusually hot for February, and the day before "the Chief Hamster," Dick Boisvert, from Concord, New Hampshire, had bought popsicles for both crews.

The Hamster Pit was a tough place to dig. The dirt "was like a sidewalk mixed with bubblegum." And yet they had found six Clovis points while they were there, and were feeling pretty good about themselves. Then John Edsal (known as "Bonedaddy") and Ed Borus, two volunteers, found a slender piece of bone. "Look at this!" they called, pointing toward the bone with their trowels. The A&M flag crackled in the light breeze. "Dang! Is that flag still higher than ours?" they called, continuing the long-running jibe between the two crews.

The bone was so crumbly it would have to be jacketed in plaster before it could be removed. The Hamsters finished up quickly and cleaned their hands. They had to get to the airport in Austin in less than two hours, so

12,500 Years Ago

Seti launched the dart with her atlatl and held her breath as it flew. Thonk! A solid hit in a small deer. The deer took off running, jumping and twisting this way and that, trying to dislodge the dart piercing its flesh. Suddenly the doe dropped to the ground and lay heaving. Seti ran to it and put her face close to the deer's nose and mouth. "Thank you, Dear Sister, for giving your life. Your breath is my breath, your heart, mine."

She placed her hand on the deer's neck as the pulsing vein stilled. She jiggled the dart sideways to loosen the grip and then pulled the point out. She had used a sharp, smooth bone point, as most women and older children learning to hunt did. These were excellent at puncturing the hide and muscle of smaller animals such as rabbits or deer. Let the men boast of mammoths; these small animals most often fed the bellies of the clan.

they had to hustle. As is the case with many interesting archaeological finds, they had found the bone in the last hour of their last day in the field.

Dick Boisvert was an old friend of Mike Collins. In fact, Collins had been Dick's advisor at the University of Kentucky, and they had worked together in France. Dick brought volunteers from New Hampshire and other states to work at the Gault site for nine years. Many of the same people came for seven or eight years, and they all paid their own way. Most had to take vacation days to come. But when you've got the archaeology bug, that's often what you do. Ten to twenty people came each year to enjoy the balmy Texas winters and have fun digging together. They camped out in tents and enjoyed the outdoors—until one year when it snowed four inches and their tents blew down. They all had to make a fast trip to Walmart for sweaters and jackets. After that, they opted to come in May.

Dick was the head of the New Hampshire State Conservation and Rescue Archaeology Program (SCRAP). His volunteers worked all over the United

The "Texas Blizzard of 2010" froze out the Hamsters in their warm-weather tents. More than one opted for indoor accommodations that night.

States "and two foreign countries—Texas and Quebec." Generally they loved coming to the Gault site because "it was an opportunity to work on an amazing site, and it's a nice place to go," especially during New England winters. Then came the snowstorm of 2010. "There's a photo of me hauling five-gallon buckets of soil to the water screen that day," Dick explained. "I'm wearing a parka and beard. We needed damn parkas to work in. We looked like the Perry Expedition after they ate the dogs."

The SCRAP volunteers didn't find out much about the piece of bone they discovered until much later, which is often the case in archaeology. There's an old maxim that for every one day in the field, it takes at least three days in the lab to properly document, curate, and identify a day's worth of artifacts, but Clark says it's actually more like thirty to forty days. Lab work typically goes on for several years after every archaeological excavation. After the bone was encased in plaster, it was taken to the Texas Archeological Research Lab at UT Austin. From there, it was sent to another lab that had more experience analyzing Pleistocene bone. Unfortunately the bone was lost at some point in the transition. Stuff happens. We can decry the situation, but things sometimes get lost, no matter who is dealing with them.

Andy Hemmings of Florida Atlantic University is a specialist in Ice Age bone tools. Unlike most archaeologists, however, Andy spends much of his time underwater rather than digging in the dirt. He has investigated some fine archaeological sites found underwater in the bottoms of clear Florida rivers. Fortunately Andy had a brief opportunity to study the Gault bone before its disappearance. According to him, the bone was probably part of a bone dart point used for hunting. The piece of the artifact that was found was about five centimeters long, probably a midsection fragment near the tip of the dart. By the size of the bone, it may have been from a deer, although definitive identification is not possible.

"I suspect this was a straight, shorter point used on the end of an atlatl-launched dart. It was not a foreshaft and I would think it was too small in diameter and length to have been a spearpoint either. When we see evidence of Paleoindian bone or ivory tool manufacture typically a long bone or tusk is splintered and the final shape is formed by hand grinding the bone," he explained.

Clovis-age bone and ivory tools have been found from Texas to Wyoming to Ohio, but the majority have been found in riverbeds in Florida, due to unusual preservation conditions. Bone was probably a common material for toolmaking thirteen thousand years ago but is only now being recognized by archaeologists and others. Hemmings believes it is likely that both bone and stone points were used during the same period, but for different purposes. He examined 137 bone and ivory Clovis tools collected from 72 sites in North America, and identified many different functional types of bone tools, such as points, daggers, billets, awls, rods, atlatl hooks, gravers, flutes, shaft tools, at least one bone wrench, and a bone handle.

Hemmings also has extensive experience recreating Clovis-like bone tools in order to understand how they were made. Bone does not fracture like chert, so there is little breakage during manufacture, which is a great advantage. Instead, bone tools were made by (1) pecking, girdling, and snapping to break off a piece the desired length; (2) stripping off the outer rough layers on tusks; and (3) grinding for finishing. A modern attempt to make a dagger from a modern horse metatarsal produced a tool in about three hours of grinding. Some bone tools, such as awls, were used for weaving plant fiber rather than hunting.

"Bone and ivory tools have almost no failure during manufacture," Andy explained, "in part due to the use of only fresh bone." Prehistoric tools were made from fresh bones because dry bones will splinter. Andy tried making bone tools from dry, weathered bones, and found them to be too brittle to work. Clovis bone and ivory tools are known to have been made from at least six animal species, including extinct llama, horse, mastodon, mammoth, wolf, and white-tailed deer. Tusks, teeth, mandibles, patella, fibula, tibia, and humerus bones were used in the past for toolmaking. These elements yield little meat, whereas bones associated with high meat density were not used for tools.

While bone and ivory are not as versatile as stone, they are more reliable for tools. Bone and ivory points are very effective at puncturing soft tissue. Bone points can be thrown on the end of a dart, or thrust into an animal. Stone points can cause more damage to tissue of an animal, but they are brittle and often break. Bone points cause less damage but do not break. "While not necessarily effective cutting weapons, they are incredibly effective at puncturing flesh," Hemmings pointed out.

Through Andy's research, the crumbling piece of bone found in the Hamster Pit has lead to a greater understanding of how Clovis-age people used the resources they had available. Almost nothing went to waste because anything they needed was eaten, processed in some manner, or stockpiled for a later time. They used everything they found in their environment. Their intimate knowledge of the land—where every plant grew and when it ripened, where every stream and spring was located, which habitat was favored by certain birds or insects—gave these people a complex mental map of things they could use to eat and survive. Researchers have learned how pieces of chert were made and used by earlier humans at the Gault site. They have also learned that mammoths and other animals encroached rather closely on this human occupational area from time to time. The unusual bone tool tells even more about Clovis ways of life. Still other evidence pointing to Clovis culture at Gault is the myriad of engraved stones found there.

Stones with a Message

In addition to the ones found by David Olmstead, more than 120 engraved or incised stones and fragments thereof have been recovered from Gault. Many were found in the early years of the project in the backdirt or other disturbed areas. Some are as small as a thumbnail, while others are about the size of the palm of your hand. Some have engraving in the cortex, or exterior of limestone or chert, and were then flaked along the edges. Most of the faint lines of engraving are straight or parallel or checkerboard.

Volunteers from the Travis County Archeological Society recovered two bits of incised stone from a screen in August 1999. Project director Jon Lohse wrote that day, "This piece shows clear geometric incising in a pattern nearly identical to at least one other stone already recovered from this site. This stone may be one of the most intricately incised we've recovered in situ from the site. Unfortunately we don't have tighter temporal resolution than Early Archaic–Late PaleoIndian."

May Schmidt found several engraved stones on the surface during her many weekends of work. "I was fascinated by the engraved stones. The stones are important, even if they do someday prove to be just doodles. After

One of the incised stones found at Gault clearly showing paired parallel lines forming a herringbone pattern. The overlying accretion occurred long after the engraving.

all, you only doodle what you know from your own culture. These stones were meaningful to the people who made them. They were trying to communicate something about what they saw or believed to someone else. So these stones are telling us about that culture."

According to Clark Wernecke, incised stones are found on every continent except Antarctica, going back 400,000 years. For example, more than 5,000 have been discovered at Parpallo Cave in Spain. More than 450 have been recovered from Gatecliff Rockshelter in Nevada. In North America, incised stones have been found in quantity in Alaska, California, the Great Basin area, and Texas, but individual stones or small numbers of them have been found throughout the continent. Investigators do not know the meaning of the scratches on the stones, but they were done on purpose. Were the stones meant to tell stories of the gods? Were they astronomical charts? Were they amulets for protection or love? We may never know. But we suspect that the marks conveyed important meaning for the people who made them.

Many types of everyday things that surely would have been used by people during the Clovis era have not been found at Gault, however. These include cordage, matting, basketry, and other items made of plant material, fabric, or skins. We can surmise that Clovis-era people must have made cord, or string, from various plant materials, based on other discoveries in different places. For example, in the dry caves of the Chihuahuan Desert in Southwest Texas, twisted cordage and matting made from yucca or sotol leaves dating back more than nine thousand years has been recovered. People who lived there wove delicate cord into mesh baskets for carrying innumerable objects, and used the string to tie on hats and other things. They wove mats for beds and living areas and made sandals from plant fibers. There is no reason to think the Clovis-era people living in Central Texas would not have done the same thing. Unfortunately there is just no direct evidence concerning this today. Many items of daily life during Clovis times have turned to dust, no longer able to share their secrets. But stone, and sometimes bone, lasts for eons. It is no surprise that the primary clues we have about some of the oldest people on the continent are made of these materials.

The discoveries of the toolmaking workshop, bone spearpoint, the mammoth bones, and the engraved stones at Gault served to build the case for Clovis period occupation along the creek. Few archaeological projects have the luxury of time (twenty-six years) and people (the hundreds of volunteers who kept coming back) to dig so meticulously or to continue to the bottom, no matter how long it takes.

May and Jim Schmidt each put in around eight hundred hours working at Gault. They did it "for the sheer knowledge gained," she admitted. "This was a great experience for volunteers. Using volunteers was great for the project, too, because since we weren't getting paid, we could take half-a-day to uncover a point if we needed to. We could afford to be meticulous. It's rare to get an opportunity to work at such a site. And it was literally all volunteers at first."

The soil around Buttermilk Creek tenderly protected the bits and flotsam of forgotten human activity for thousands of years. Today artifacts from Gault are curated for the future in a climate-controlled building. College students, professional archaeologists, and volunteers move trays of chert or bone fragments to long tables to study under microscopes, hoping one day to understand more about the people who lived millennia before us.

4 Gault since Clovis

We do not have a defined interval in Central Texas
history that is not represented at Gault.

—MIKE COLLINS

Gault Today

Today the Gault site is a designated State Antiquities Landmark and is listed
in the National Register of Historic Places. The Lindsey family still lives on
the original farm. Their normal comings and goings are the only activity
most days. In 2007 they sold part of the land containing most of the prehistoric remains to Dr. Collins, who donated it to the Archaeological Conservancy. The archaeological site is now protected in perpetuity. Cars and
pickups and gravel trucks swoosh down the paved county road in front of
the farm. Rock quarries grind wet slabs of limestone all day long within hear-
ing distance. Tour groups tromp along the path with volunteers from the
Gault School for Archaeological Research (GSAR). Birds sing in the trees,
and water flows in the creek.

Recent Past (1870–2007)

Henry Clay Gault was born in 1870 in a log cabin about thirty miles north
of Austin, Texas. During his lifetime, Henry Clay managed to acquire various pieces of property not far from the old homestead. One of the places
was the fertile little valley along Buttermilk Creek near Florence where he

raised cotton and grew vegetables. After his wife died in 1942, he sold the place to Nealy Lindsey and moved in with his daughter. Even after almost eighty years of different ownership, Henry Clay's farm is still known as the Gault place.

His grandfather, John McCain Gault, came to Texas from Tennessee sometime between 1838 and 1840 during the land rush days of the Texas Republic. It is likely that in 1850 he built a cabin in an area still inhabited by Tonkawas and occasional raiding Comanches, a few miles north of the newly established town of Austin. The property was owned at the time by J. P. Whelin, a veteran of the Texas Army in the war for independence from Mexico.

Whelin had served in the Texas Army for three months, from May to August 1836. The war was over by the time he joined, however, as Sam Houston had settled it at the Battle of San Jacinto in April. The Republic of Texas had no money to compensate the men who had served in the army, but it did have land. And it needed settlers. So a generous land giveaway program began. Thus Whelin received 320 acres for his three months' service—arguably one of the best veteran's benefits ever bestowed.

It is not known exactly how John McCain Gault acquired land from Whelin, but a patent deed in the Texas General Land Office shows that a certain parcel was patented to John M. Gault's heirs in 1901. We do know that John McCain Gault was prospering enough by 1855 to purchase other land nearby from Captain Nelson Merrill and build a larger home. Merrill, also a Texas army veteran, settled on his bounty land in 1837, just after Texas' independence from Mexico. There he operated a store, in addition to receiving the mail for other farmers. The community grew slowly and then ceased to grow altogether, and by 1902 the post office closed. Today, except for the graveyard, suburban Pflugerville has erased all evidence of Merrilltown.

John McCain's son, James Henry Gault, was born in Tennessee in 1838 and came to Texas as an infant with his momma and daddy. When he married sometime around 1865, he probably moved into John McCain's old log cabin and started his family. Henry Clay Gault was quite likely born in that same cabin five years later.

The old homestead slowly fell into ruin, and by 1980 it was being used to store hay on a cattle farm. The cabin was saved, however, when the city

The log cabin where Henry Clay Gault probably was born in 1870 is now a historical landmark near Austin.

of Austin decided to restore the frontier home, now in a new subdivision, as the centerpiece of Katherine Fleischer Park. Thus the log cabin where Henry Clay was born became a window on the pioneer past of more than 150 years ago, just as his farm a few miles away became an aperture into the ancient past of 13,000 years ago. Henry Clay's farm is now known as the Gault archaeological site, and it is changing the way scholars see the entire peopling of the Americas.

The first archaeological investigation of the Gault site was made by J. E. Pearce in 1929. Pearce was head of the new Department of Anthropology at the University of Texas in Austin. Archaeology was still a new field at the time, and the methods of excavation were lackadaisical by today's standards. The only records of the work are a few photographs and two short reports. His crew recovered over three thousand artifacts, seventy-eight of which were traded to the Penn Museum, now called the University of Pennsylvania Museum of Archaeology and Anthropology. Today the majority of the artifacts are housed at the Texas Archeological Research Laboratory at the University of Texas.

Historic Inhabitants at Gault (1600–1870)

Several historic visitors to the Gault area left crude initials incised in a band of chert, and one drew a facsimile of a church, perhaps denoting contact with American, European, or African peoples sometime during the late 1700s. During the period from 1600 to 1870, Tonkawa, Comanche, and other tribes frequented the area near the Gault site.

Historians have identified Tonkawas and Comanches in Central Texas primarily through historic records. For example, there are numerous written accounts of encounters with members of both groups from the mid-1700s forward. In those days, both tribes were nomadic buffalo hunters who used bows and arrows, spears, and rifles they obtained from Spanish, French, or Anglo traders and others. They wore buckskin leggings or short skirts with buffalo robes for added warmth in the winter. Leaders, or chiefs, in both groups were chosen by the elders of the band or tribe.

The Tonkawa were a confederation of smaller bands, and their name itself literally means "they all stay together." The tribe acquired horses at some point, possibly from Spanish traders or other Indian groups. They lived in tepees made from buffalo hide or brush arbors. Their culture was similar to many Plains Indian tribes. Besides buffalo, they also ate small game, fish, nuts like acorns and pecans, and plant foods such as berries, seeds, and wild fruits. They wore distinctive tattoos and held extensive funeral rites. The people were matrilineal, meaning the children belonged to the mother and men lived with their mate's band.

The dirt around Buttermilk Creek was churned up for fifty years or more in the twentieth century by relic collectors who paid to dig on the site, hoping to recover a Comanche or Tonkawa arrowhead. And find things they did. There is no estimate of how many projectile points from Gault are now hanging on living room walls in decorative arrays. The top layers of soil at Gault were so dug into and mixed up by enthusiastic shovelers that they are not particularly useful to archaeologists. Remains from historic inhabitants became so jumbled that accurate archaeological dating of such items is nearly impossible.

Between 1746 and 1756, the Spanish established three short-lived missions on the San Gabriel River for the Tonkawa near the present-day town of Rockdale. In 1758, however, the Tonkawa joined with Comanches and

A hummingbird rests on the outstretched hand of a worker at Gault. Close encounters with nature are one of the treats of archaeology.

other tribes to raid Mission San Saba, about eighty-five miles northwest. The mission there was burned and the priests massacred. After that, the Spanish did not attempt to convert the Tonkawa again. Stephen F. Austin entered into a treaty with the tribe in 1824 to ease Anglo colonization of Texas. The Republic of Texas made certain agreements with them in 1837 and 1838. By 1854, the Tonkawa were dying from European diseases and the loss of the buffalo herds due to drought and overhunting. By 1855, Tonkawa survivors were expelled to Indian Territory in present-day Oklahoma.

The Comanches were mounted raiders who came to Texas sometime prior to the eighteenth century. They were expert horsemen who hunted buffalo and lived in tepees that could easily be moved from place to place. The Penateka band, or "Honey Eaters," lived on the plains in Central Texas, in the area roughly west of Interstate Highway 35 today, as well as other places. Buffalo provided food, clothing, and shelter for the people. The Comanche often traded buffalo robes, horses, and captives with other tribes on the Southern Plains. Horses were a measure of wealth to the Comanche, and were often stolen back and forth in raids. Each tribal group elected both peace chiefs and war chiefs, but the peace chief was the most influential.

In 1785 the Spanish concluded a treaty with the Comanches concerning Spanish settlements in Texas. Conditions deteriorated in 1824, however, when Anglo settlers began to intrude into Comanche territory. In 1836 Comanches raided Fort Parker and took a young girl named Cynthia Ann captive. She lived with the Comanches for twenty-four years and married Peta Nokona, a chief. They had three children, including the last free Comanche chief, Quanah Parker. Anglos recaptured her in 1860 and forced her to leave her Indian family. She died of heartbreak, it is said, several years later.

By 1854 the Penatekas had been decimated by the depletion of the buffalo herds, disease, and warfare. Survivors were moved to a reservation near present-day Throckmorton, Texas, and five years later pushed onto a reservation in Indian Territory. Raids on settlers did not cease, however, and other Comanche bands held absolute control in West Texas. The Treaty of Medicine Lodge in 1867 failed to change the situation. In the Red River War of 1874, the last Comanches in Texas were defeated by the US Army in the Battle of Palo Duro Canyon. All the Comanche horses were killed and the people's tepees burned. The survivors straggled into Indian Territory soon thereafter.

Late Prehistoric (1000–1600)

The first written record about Texas was the account by Cabeza de Vaca, a Spaniard who was shipwrecked on the Texas coast in 1528. He wandered through south Texas and northern Mexico for eight years before reaching Mexico City in 1536. He chronicled many Native American groups that he encountered, sometimes by name, after his return to Spain. Before this time, we do not know the names of the many peoples who lived in Texas, such as those along Buttermilk Creek.

Archaeologists refer to the general culture in Central Texas during the latter part of the Late Prehistoric period as *Toyah*. Distinctive features of this cultural style included specific types of stone tools, ceramic pots, and bison hunting. Use of the bow and arrow is reflected in the type of projectile points used. Small arrowpoints from this period known as Perdiz points are widely distributed across Texas, Louisiana, and northern Mexico. They were a key component of the Toyah tool kit. Besides hunting with bows and ar-

Wet conditions from a high water table were a constant problem at Gault. Here water has collected in the haphazard burrows of arrowhead hunters.

rows tipped with Perdiz points, the people also used beveled stone knives for butchering, and end scrapers for working hides and other materials.

As mentioned, the top layers of dirt along Buttermilk Creek were badly disturbed over the years by hobbyists looking for loot. Many Late Prehistoric artifacts were taken from Gault and are now sitting in shoeboxes at the back of people's closets or on the walls of their living rooms.

During the period from 1300 to 1500, bison returned to Central Texas after an absence of about 1,500 years. Many bison bones have been discovered at archaeological sites, including Gault, from this era, and some archaeologists have characterized people of that time as bison hunters. People also used earth ovens layered with hot stones to bake or steam tough plant foods such as yucca bulbs. These earth ovens can be seen all over Central Texas today as big mounds of burned limestone. Research has shown that people reused these ovens over and over, sometimes for centuries. A large earth oven mound at Gault was about 90 percent destroyed by hobbyists long before archaeological work began in the 1990s.

Only two small fragments of pottery were found by Collins and his team, each about the size of a fingernail. People started making this particular kind of pottery around 1300. Prior to this time, hunter-gatherers in this area did not have pottery, even though groups in other parts of North America had been making pottery for centuries. Central Texas potters made simple earthenware pottery with clay, to which they often added pulverized animal bone. They decorated some vessels with a red-ochre slip or simple incised decorations. Generally the pots were utilitarian such as water jugs and bowls. This bone-tempered pottery was fired at very low temperatures, broke easily, and weathered badly over time. Archaeologists typically find only small potsherds at sites, and whole or reconstructable vessels are rare.

In addition, blade technology reminiscent of Clovis for making stone tools reappears in the region around 1300 after an absence of over 12,500 years, although these blades were much smaller and more irregular in shape. Not all Central Texas groups adopted blade technology, but many did and they probably did so mainly because this flintknapping technique allowed toolmakers to produce more useful pieces with suitable cutting edges than was possible with conventional flintknapping methods. Archaeologists are unsure why this technology reappeared after such a long absence.

Toyah culture is not yet well understood by archaeologists. Identifiers include a unique set of things seen over a two- or three-century period across much of the southern half of Texas, including the area where Gault is located. This material culture was adopted by many different social/ethnic groups who may not have shared much else in common. The relationships among this culture and the earliest Indian groups that Europeans encountered in the sixteenth century are not clear. Archaeologists still have many questions about the people who lived four to seven hundred years ago in North America, which is one reason it is important to preserve ancient occupational sites until modern research techniques can be applied to unlock their secrets.

Archaic Period (8000 BCE–1000 CE)

In other parts of the Western Hemisphere, people were evolving different sorts of cultures prior to 1 CE. Somewhere between 2000 and 500 BCE, ancient people in the North American Southwest began to cultivate maize and live in pit houses dug into the ground. In the Mississippi and Ohio

River systems, certain groups built earthen mounds for various purposes. Watson-Brake archaeological site in Louisiana is an impressive multimound site built more than 5,400 years ago. It is considered to be the oldest mound complex in North America, and may have played an important ceremonial role. Starting about 3,000 years ago, the Maya in Central America were also building earthen mounds, plus they were farming corn, squash, and beans, and creating complex societies.

None of this was the case during the Archaic period stretching from 8000 BCE to 1000 CE in Central Texas near Buttermilk Creek. There, people were nomadic hunter-gatherers who moved several times a year in search of food and other resources, such as firewood. The climate was somewhat drier than it was at the end of the last Ice Age, and the Pleistocene animals were gone. They were replaced by the modern buffalo, antelope, and deer, as well as many small mammals. People hunted these animals with a dart and atlatl, often called a spear thrower, an ingenious device that increases the distance a dart can be thrown. When thrown with an atlatl, a dart point acts like a spring, flexing and compressing as it flies. This results in speeds up to one hundred miles per hour. Recent experiments have shown that darts thrown with atlatls can easily pierce half-inch plywood.

People used earth ovens dug in shallow pits in the ground and filled with hot rocks to cook certain plant foods, especially roots and bulbs, to increase their food value and make them palatable. As noted previously, these cooking features are scattered everywhere in Central Texas. Think of roasting a pig in a pit in the backyard, and you have the idea.

People often traded resources, such as stone tools, with other groups they encountered. We have no direct evidence of trade in perishable goods during this period, but likely people also traded baskets, hides, feathers, ochre, nuts, and other things.

People during this long period of time lived in small bands of extended family with perhaps twenty-five people in one group. They were affiliated with other bands or tribes in some fashion, but exactly how is not known. People from various bands came together from time to time to trade and choose mates. We have no evidence concerning marriage per se, but it is likely that everyone in the band looked after children and helped contribute food to the group in some way. Children, who often died before the age of five, would have been precious. (Some anthropological accounts of modern hunter-gatherers disagree, however, contending that emotional bonds with infants are too painful in societies where infant mortality is high.) Children would have been needed to carry on particular traditions of each band, such as venerating ancestors, as well as helping gather food and firewood.

Likely these hunter-gatherers wore modest clothing made of deer hide or woven grasses. Certain plants had leaves suitable for weaving things such as mats or capes. Some may have stitched tanned rabbit skins together with sinew or cordage to make capes and hats. Bone awls have been found that indicate punching holes in leather and other materials, as might be needed for sewing.

Technological change was slow, but manufacturing strategies did evolve. Stemmed dart points of various types were used during this period, spanning nine thousand years or so. A new heat treatment for chert was developed that made good chert even better. The heating improved the "flakability" of the material and gave it a higher luster, according to lithic technologist Sergio Ayala. "There's lots of moisture in chert," he said. "Heat evaporates the moisture, but also draws out other stuff. We are still trying to figure out the chemical process."

This Archaic period is a "hell of a lot more complex than we previously believed," Sergio noted. "The more you get into it the more you see. [We see] potential relationships to ecological change and social change."

The Gault project recovered artifacts from every time period since Clovis, and has curated them for future analysis. The fact that these different bits of rock and a few other things could be found in different layers of the soil around Buttermilk Creek, getting older the farther down the crew dug, proves that thinking, breathing people chose to live there over and over again through the millennia. Likely knowledge of this excellent location was widespread among the seminomadic people of the times, as were many other locales. People might tell their kin to meet them there at certain times of year to gather nuts, sharpen spearpoints, placate the gods, and perform other ceremonies. For more than sixteen thousand years, somebody has always lived in the shade of the trees along the little stream. Now archaeologists are beginning to piece together the puzzle of these ancient lifeways and construct a more profound understanding of these pioneers in North America.

5 Something Even Older

Sometime around 15,000 Years Ago

Mikasi was struggling to notch a spear to hold the small new stone point he had proudly made, but the wood kept splitting and the spear shaft grew shorter and shorter with each failure. "Ugh! Maybe I should just start over." He stopped a moment and looked at his cousin and clanmate, Dohate. They had grown up together and lived in the same small band all their lives.

"Do you have another shaft for a new spear?" asked Dohate.

"No, I'll have to go try to find a nut tree limb—the straight ones are getting scarce around here." Mikasi carefully wrapped the curiously small projectile point with a smooth piece of hide and tucked it away in his hunting bag.

"I'll come with you," said Dohate. He began to sing about the great animal spirits, and soon Mikasi joined in as they headed down the valley toward the nut tree grove.

Something even older than Clovis was waiting for modern researchers at Gault in September 2007. In a section called Area 15, under the watchful eye of Mike Collins, after six and a half years of intermittent work, volunteers discovered strange-looking stone artifacts that looked nothing like the Clovis specimens. They opened up a forty-eight square meter area that narrowed down into twelve square meters at bedrock. They had shored up the sides with wood and built several steps into the pit. The lower excavation was about the size of a small living room in a modern-day house. They had dug it primarily using small pointed bamboo skewers, or splints, so as not to accidentally break anything hidden in the dirt. Deep in the silty clay lay many Clovis period artifacts, and below that was a layer of sterile deposits. That is, for a depth of about fifteen centimeters, very few artifacts of any kind were found. Then, suddenly, below that barren layer, workers began to find things that had clearly been made by woman and man, but didn't look anything like Clovis.

Cinda Timperly works with a bamboo skewer to prevent damage to any potential artifact. Much of the earth removal at Gault was painstaking and slow.

About 150,000 pieces of human-modified rock, including about 80 tools and 149,020 chert flakes, were recovered from this lowest layer before hitting bedrock. Workers pulled out a few stemmed tools that might have once been hafted to wooden darts. Beneath them was nothing but solid rock. The workers had hit the bottom of the earth's soil. The bits and chips of worked stone they found were left there by ancient people from an unknown culture. The workers at Gault were discovering the remains of a totally unknown people who lived more than fifteen thousand years ago. In fact, the sediment on the bedrock beneath the "older than Clovis" (OTC) materials has returned at least one date of about twenty-two thousand years ago. If the OTC dates hold after further scientific scrutiny, they will rewrite the story of mankind in the Americas.

The workers had discovered something OTC. That wasn't supposed to happen, according to some archaeologists' thinking. In fact, if you had asked most archaeologists during the past seventy years, they would have told you that this just couldn't be true. But it's just what Mike Collins, the man who loved dirt, had surmised all along.

"We knew we had OTC," Mike explained. "That's what I had been looking for all along. It was a purposeful search. I was always looking for hints, clues, evidence that might expand the story (of early people in the Western Hemisphere). The Bering Strait/Clovis First model seemed too pat to me, too improbable.

"Around thirteen thousand years ago many sites in Texas were scoured of alluvial deposits. There wasn't any older dirt, only bedrock. I began to look for places where the dirt had not been scoured out. Gault is one of those places. There, an enormous amount of dirt holds that record. This was the kind of thing I'd been looking for."

Mike knew dirt. His study of geology and archaeology in many parts of the world had taught him what to look for in order to find evidence of early inhabitants in the North American continent. He was elated when the crew finally got down deep enough to break through Clovis and see what, if anything, was underneath. The first chert flakes recovered from this layer were astounding to Mike. He studied the flakes carefully to see how the stones were fractured. And there it was: the unmistakable genius of thinking, planning humankind.

Mike's field journal for June 24, 2000, reveals: "We are in tan clay with $CaCO_3$ [calcium carbonate]. This is the unit that we believe to underlie Clovis. Our objective is the gleyed clay w/artifacts beneath the tan clay."

"Gleyed" is a geologic term meaning a sticky waterlogged soil that lacks oxygen, typically gray to blue in color. This dirt plays an important role in the OTC story at Gault, because scientists were actually able to get a date on the dirt itself. Since there was no charcoal or other organic material for radiocarbon dating, another method had to be used. This was optically stimulated luminescence (OSL), a method of dating tiny mineral grains such as quartz or feldspar in soil. Because the technique uses the physics of ionizing radiation, the results are considered accurate, though not precise. There is a fairly large margin of error with this methodology. Events that can be dated this way include the mineral's last exposure to radiation or sunlight. In other words, scientists can determine when a column of dirt taken from twelve feet underground, for example, last saw daylight.

If the soil has not been disturbed, OSL techniques indicate when that sand grain was last on top of the ground. According to Clark, it is very unlikely that the OTC stemmed points were stratigraphically disturbed (i.e., that they had moved up or down within the soil). "Never say never," he said, "but we see no indications of any mixing and, in fact, have multiple lines of evidence to show the lowest strata are undisturbed."

By the magic of OSL technology, experts found that the lowest layer of soil they sampled from Gault had last seen the light of day approximately sixteen to eighteen thousand years ago. Likely that means the simple stone tools embedded in that layer of soil were that old as well, although this is still subject to further testing. If these dates can be cross-verified, this discovery considerably pushes back the period of known human occupation in the American continents. Until very recently, few would have believed that possible.

This discovery was the culmination of many years of work, and Mike was eager to keep going. But that didn't happen. Fieldwork halted abruptly in the end of May 2002 when the landowners decided not to renew the lease with Mike. They wanted to build a house on the land and enjoy peace and quiet instead, and who could blame them? They had been periodically infested with swarms of volunteers and professional archaeologists for almost ten years. It would be seven more years before Mike and his crew could come back to realize their dream. In the meantime, materials from Gault were cleaned and stored, waiting for analysis.

After five years of unsuccessful negotiation, Mike made a deal with the landowner to buy the property outright in February 2007. Citizen scientists came back to work side by side with professionals, on hands and knees, digging sticky, waterlogged soil with little pointed sticks to recover precious chips of ancient stone. They pulled large, crude bifaces and strange, small, stemmed projectile points from the dirt lying below the Clovis soil layer, as well as a number of flake tools.

Only a few projectile point bases or stems, about the size of your thumb, have been identified as OTC projectile points. They look like projectile points, and at least two of the points were hafted, or attached to handles by using some kind of sticky glue-like substance and tying, probably with animal sinew. There are two different base shapes, which have been ground. Grinding dulls the edge of the point so it will not cut through the sinew for hafting.

These artifacts from Gault are considered older than Clovis and date back to more than fifteen thousand years ago. The people of that time made a variety of stone tools for different purposes.

Nancy Williams believes the people who lived in this area before Clovis times were hunter-gatherers who visited the little creek seasonally. They evidently were processing a lot of food and hides. They used sharp chert flakes to cut meat off bones, and probably cut it into strips to dry. They scraped remains off animal hides to clean them before drying and tanning for use. They cut plants of various kinds, perhaps reeds that grew along the stream, to make shelters or matting. They scraped wood, perhaps to make spears or for other uses. Maybe in Central Texas ancient people didn't have to be on the move constantly because there was plenty of game, plants, water, and of course good chert, right there on Buttermilk Creek. We know the Gault site was intensely occupied, with never a break for very long.

"Archaeologists take notes so they can put the site back together through analysis," said Nancy. The difference between archaeologists and arrowhead hunters is that "arrowhead hunters only get a small bit of the picture. We want to give everyone the entire story."

Marilyn Shoberg, a specialist in use-wear, or the extremely light scaring left on tools that have been used for cutting and other activities, analyzed more than six hundred stone artifacts from Gault, forty of which were from the older than Clovis layer. She found that the tools had been used for butchering, cutting soft animal tissue, cutting reeds, cutting wood, planing wood, scraping wood, cutting hide, cutting bone, and piercing soft tissue, perhaps for scarification or tattooing. "While the artifacts made of plant, bone and animal skin have not survived the thousands of years since they were discarded at the Gault site, we know from the stone tools they used that the people there were making the essential things needed for their complex lives," she explains.

The initial assumption about these oldest artifacts was that OTC stone working would be similar to Clovis. Nancy spent five years closely analyzing these flakes and tools in the GSAR lab at Texas State University. To her surprise, "[They're] not at all like Clovis. But perhaps Clovis developed from this. The blade technology is very similar," she says, "but the biface technology is very different. Clovis uses a well-developed flaking system, but OTC appears to be just competent, not quite as bold, more random, just getting by." When you see the assemblage, even an untrained eye can tell the difference. The older than Clovis stuff just looks different.

Jennifer Gandy studies the tiniest of chert flakes under a microscope in order to classify them in various ways. She's counted and weighed them by size. Indeed, the chert flakes are various colors from brown to gray, some streaked, some occluded, some rough, some smooth as glass. Some are the size of a thumbnail, others larger than an adult's hand. The OTC material is not quite as pretty as Clovis, according to Jennifer:

> The OTC flakes are slightly cruder than Clovis and the platforms look like less time was spent on them. They're not as narrow as Clovis. The flakes are smaller in size than Clovis ones, too. Of course these are initial observations, and they may change as we learn more. I still have a lot to learn, but I can really see differences after a while. We can tell as much if not more from the flakes as we can the tools. We can see the mind of the creator of the tools, the decisions that were made.

In other words, she can see how the original flintknapper chipped off the flakes, how he or she made decisions about where to hit the rock, and how hard. These subtle clues are meaningful to experts who seek to learn the secrets of how ancient things were made. The differences in OTC and Clovis flakes may in time give us a better understanding of the human adventurers who lived by the creek so many thousands of years ago.

The Cobblestone Floor

It was October 2001, and the crew had been carefully removing layers of soil from a fairly level area a bit farther away from the creek since February. They were finally down to the layer where they thought Clovis-era materials might be found. One excavator was working with a trowel when she began to come down on a layer of small limestone cobbles. *Nothing too unusual—could be part of a gravel bar long covered by pasture*, she thought. But then her pal in another corner of the unit hit pebbles, too. "OK, just clean the tops off and be careful about flakes or anything lying on top or wedged in between," she said to her friend. Slowly they continued scraping dirt in the early fall heat. They were on their hands and knees, arms tan, sunscreen slathered on the backs of their necks. The hats they wore were so dirty their mothers

15,000 Years Ago

Pamuy leaned on her stick to survey the camp. In most years this was a hospitable place and the people were happy to come here. Huge pecan and walnut trees spread their dense shade along the creek banks. Ohcumgache sat under a tree with several other men making fresh spearpoints and knives for future work. The gray stone here was particularly good and could be gotten without much effort. A short rise between the stream and the uplands was made almost entirely of exposed chert. Sometimes chunks fell off and could be easily picked up. More often the men and boys gathered suitable pieces that had tumbled down the streambed from farther away. The gray stone broke into sharp, shiny flakes when struck just right with a hammerstone. Tools made from the gray chert were strong and sharp—valuable qualities for hunters.

Farther down, girls carried bundles of grass to replenish the beds in the sleeping area. Pamuy's daughter, Taipa, scraped meat off the bones of a large animal, preparing it to dry over the fire overnight. Boys were romping near the creek, turning over rocks and splashing. Perhaps they would find crayfish to eat. Someone—it looked like Tokala from the back—was hacking on a log, maybe for a timber for the new structure. The old one had been severely damaged by last spring's flood, and great trouble had come to the people. The shaman decided that the shrine for the sacred masks had to be moved to ward off evil spirits. She even demanded that stones be carried in to form a solid floor to keep water from seeping up from the ground.

Uncovering and recognizing the gravel floor at Gault called for precise measurements and documentation. Each stone was mapped in place, and workers went shoeless to avoid damaging stones.

would have made them throw them out. Humidity rose up from the ground around them, and sweat soaked their clothes.

It wasn't until the next weekend that the two young women saw the rocks make a right turn. "Huh," one said. "I'd better show this to Clark," who was overseeing several units out in the field that day. "Clark, get over here," she yelled.

He looked up from his clipboard and came loping over. A baseball cap gave little shade to his sun-warmed face. "What's up?" he said.

The two women bent down in the hole straightened up to take a break. "Take a look at this."

Clark squinted at the whitish pebbles that had been meticulously scraped clean by the diggers. Some were about the size of baseballs, but many others were tiny, like gravel scooped from a gravel bar. "Huh," he said. "Well, I guess we've got to follow this line on out and see where it goes. Just keep going like you're doing until you find the end."

The two volunteers in the hole looked at each other. "OK. Will do," they said, gamely. After all, this is what they'd come for that Saturday—to dig in the dirt and maybe find a trace of something old. Some life from before they could even imagine. Some trace of a person almost like them, only from thousands of years ago.

By mid-October an almost square feature of small gravels two meters by two meters, with a little apse or rectangular protuberance on the north side, had been exposed by the volunteers in the unit. Mike Collins wrote in his field journal for October 20, 2001:

> As shown in sketch at right, the rectangular feature also has a number of large rocks in it and mostly around its N, W, and S sides. . . . There are very few pieces of chert inside, and somewhat more outside the rectangular patch of gravel. These include flakes, blades and at least one biface fragment. There were blades and a biface fragment removed from unit near the southwest corner before this feature was recognized. We speculate that this might be a hut floor later covered w/grass and/ or hides. There is no evidence of a superstructure. . . .
>
> *If* this feature is the remains of a domestic structure, the fact that the larger stones are to the outer perimeter suggests their use as weights or support post chocks; that the chipped stone is mostly outside is analogous to the pottery seen in Magdalenian huts.

Mike was thinking of the traces of grass and animal hide huts in France from 12,000 to 17,000 years ago that he had once studied. If this accumulation of gravel does prove to be the floor of a hut of some kind, it would be perhaps the oldest structural floor in North America. Recent OSL testing of sand grains from below the cobblestones has returned dates between 14,900 and 15,400 years ago, making this almost 2,000 years before the Clovis cultural manifestation.

"It's an anomaly," says Laura Vilsack, who studied the feature. "The date is extraordinary. We are on the cusp of understanding that people were here this early. [This was] made to permanently stay there. [It] doesn't match anything else exactly in North America. The closest match is in France both in size of structure and size of rocks and direction they face. The sides line up north and south. It has an apse, or entryway, facing north. Exactly facing north. Perhaps it was aligned with the stars, who knows? Very curious."

In February 2002, Mike had several visitors in the field: Thomas Stafford, Britt Bousman of Texas State University, and Ernie Lundelius, from UT

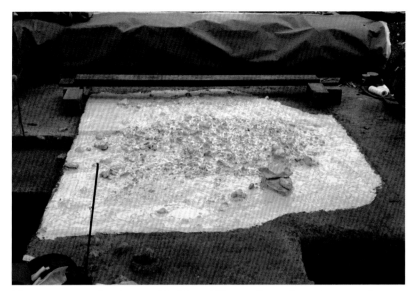

The attempt to make a latex mold of the cobblestone floor—better known as the vomit mold—eventually failed, but not without a great deal of work and effort.

Austin. The four walked the site and discussed what they were seeing in the dirt. They lingered by the uncovered stone pavement until, according to Mike, finally they "were in agreement that the stone feature was not natural." "Mostly we discussed possible functions—domicile? Burial cover? Other?" What were these stones really for? A living area? A ceremonial place? Food storage? The exact function of the stone patio will likely never be resolved, simply because there isn't enough evidence to form a solid conclusion. Nevertheless, gravel doesn't make four right angles on its own, so people must have had a hand in construction for some purpose that suited them at the time.

A few weeks later James Adovasio, best known for his work at Meadowcroft Shelter in Pennsylvania, visited the site. The deepest of the cultural layers at Meadowcroft spans sixteen to nineteen thousand radiocarbon years of sporadic human occupation, which makes it one of the oldest known sites in the Western Hemisphere. Exactly what he and Mike discussed is not recorded, but Clark pointed out that intentionally snapped segments of Clovis-like prismatic blades were found in association with the stone pavement. One can imagine the debate over beer that day after walking the field. How did the blades get there? Why were they broken? What do they mean?

Archaeologists love to bounce ideas off each other and debate any inconsistencies. That's sort of how science works. Especially in archaeology, truth is never achieved in a single moment, from a single point of view, but by trial and error, debate, and recalibration, over and over again.

Before Mike and his team were finished with the stone pavement area, they tried several times to make casts of the gravel floor. They tried to make a latex model of the stone, but a number of things went wrong, according to Clark, and a final mold was not possible.

"In the early days of laser scanning [around 2003], a group from UT was all set up to scan the floor, but failed because they didn't have the right cord to connect the laser and the computer," Clark explained. "All kinds of things went wrong, but we do have 3D photogrammetry of the floor." Using 3D photogrammetry, scientists can make measurements from photographs, especially to recover the exact positions of uneven surface points, making it excellent for recording the three-dimensional design of an ancient gravel surface.

The mystery pavement is covered up now and grass grows over it among the wildflowers. Once the archaeologists had gathered all the data they could from the strange cobblestone square, and made precise maps and other recordings of the location, they covered the exposed gravel with dirt to preserve it for future research. Perhaps one day new technologies can be applied to the old stones to bring us new insights into human behavior.

The only other known stone floor dating back to Clovis or before in North America is at Kincaid Shelter, about a week's walk south of Gault. There, limestone cobbles were carried into a rockshelter, and presumably covered with grass and animal hides to provide a comfortable living space. In the late 1980s Mike Collins studied stone tools found on the floor at Kincaid Shelter while he was with the Texas Archeological Research Laboratory at UT Austin, and found them to be unmistakably Clovis. Mike submitted charcoal samples from the floor that looked like "flecks from a pepper shaker" for dating through accelerated mass spectrometry (AMS), a great advance over standard radiocarbon dating. The results produced a date of approximately twelve thousand years old.

"Kincaid is the only site with indisputable evidence of Clovis-period construction, because there was the bone of an extinct horse lying right on top of the pavement," Mike explained. The placement of the bone collaborates

What Is 3D Photogrammetry?

Three-dimensional photogrammetry is the science of making measurements from overlapping photographs, especially for recovering the exact positions of surface points. Photogrammetry has been around since the mid-nineteenth century, but digital methods now make this a very reliable mapping tool for twenty-first century archaeologists. Photogrammetry uses methods from many fields, including optics and projective geometry. The technique is used in topographic mapping, engineering, architecture, geology, and other endeavors. Archaeologists use 3D photogrammetry to produce maps of large or complex sites as well as features and even artifacts.

with the AMS date, providing firm evidence of Clovis at Kincaid. The date of the floor at Gault is thousands of years earlier, however. The Gault discovery could indicate that human beings were living in North America much earlier than previously thought.

Other OTC Sites in the Americas

About thirty-five other sites in North America and perhaps thirty in South America are suspected of having OTC components. About three hundred meters downstream from Gault, on the same little Buttermilk Creek, lies the Debra. L. Freidkin site, investigated by Mike Waters from Texas A&M, who worked at Gault in 2000. He figured Clovis material must also be found farther down the stream, on other landowners' property. He not only found Clovis, but also more than fifteen thousand chips and tools, starting about an inch underneath the Clovis layer. This OTC layer continued for about eight inches before reaching bedrock. "This is the oldest credible archaeological site in North America," Waters said in 2011, with perhaps some hyperbole. Steven Forman from the University of Illinois, Chicago, directed OSL dating procedures for Freidkin. When the data were analyzed, they consistently yielded the same ages. "This was unequivocal proof of pre-Clovis," he said. To be fair, it must be noted that other experts have written strong critiques of this conclusion.

Possible OTC sites have also been discovered in the eastern United States. A rockshelter, known as Meadowcroft, about twenty-five miles southwest of Pittsburgh, Pennsylvania, has returned radiocarbon dates from sixteen to nineteen thousand years ago. These dates are highly controversial, however, with some archaeologists claiming contamination from ancient carbon from coal-bearing layers in the watershed. Further tests with new technologies have confirmed these early dates. If these findings hold against further testing, Meadowcroft may be the location of one of the oldest human habitations yet found in North America.

James Adovasio, who consulted at Gault, still leads the excavation at Meadowcroft, which he started in 1973. "We did not realize the depth of the deposits or its antiquity," Adovasio told the Pennsylvania Center for the Book located at Penn State University. "It was almost serendipitous. It was literally nothing anyone had anticipated."

More than twenty thousand artifacts have been recovered over thirty years of work at Meadowcroft. About five hundred pieces of material that may prove to be older than Clovis were found nearly 11.5 feet below surface. Like most other very old sites where human beings lived, this one is located just above a creek, in an area where food resources would have been plentiful. Today Meadowcroft Rockshelter and Historic Village is a National Historic Landmark with a new museum and a covered deck where visitors can look into the excavation area itself.

Excavation from 1993 to 2002 at the Cactus Hill site on the Nottoway River in Virginia recovered some remarkable charcoal near stone tools that produced both radiocarbon and OSL dates between eighteen and twenty thousand years ago. Strange stone tools unlike anything made in Clovis times were unearthed by Joseph M. McAvoy of the Nottoway River Survey and Michael T. Johnson of the Archeological Society of Virginia. The fact that the tools were so different in design led archaeologists to theorize that the people who made them were not related to the people who made Clovis tools. The material was earlier than Clovis, and completely dissimilar.

Two archaeologists point out the layers in a stratigraphic profile at the Cactus Hill site in Virginia where unusual artifacts were discovered.

In spring 2002, Mike Johnson and part of his crew visited Gault to join the work. Instead of the glorious spring weather they had anticipated, however, they were met with a cold north wind and drizzle. Before noon, the rain was too heavy to remain in the field, so they shut things down and went into Austin to the lab. There they compared the materials extracted from on top of the bedrock at Gault to the bits they had found in Virginia, raising even more questions than they had had before. Cactus Hill OTC is still controversial, but may provide another window into the earliest population of North America.

More than one hundred years ago in Vero Beach, Florida, workers enlarging a canal to bring water for the burgeoning citrus orchards hit fossilized animal bones and human-made bone projectile points. E. H. Sellards, whom we've met before, was then the State Geologist of Florida, so the bones and tools were sent to him for analysis. He identified the bones as those of Ice Age mastodons, saber-toothed cats, and giant sloths. Since the projectile points were recovered near these bones, he theorized they must be from the same time period, about fourteen thousand years ago. Of course nobody believed him at the time.

After working at Vero Beach for four years, James Adovasio presented new data to the Society for American Archeology in 2018 about these bone projectile points. Turns out, modern radiocarbon dating methods reveal that the points are only about seven thousand years old, only half as old as Sellards first surmised.

"We took a small section of the center of that point and subjected it to radio carbon dating," Adovasio told the Treasure Coast Palms (TCP) online news outlet. "Theoretically, if it was actually as old as Sellards claimed, it would have in fact been more than eleven thousand years old, and similar to the age of those extinct animals. As it turns out, that projectile point is less than seven thousand years old."

Nonetheless, Vero Beach is an amazing site, with more than fifty-three types of mammal bones found there, more than twenty of which are now extinct. "The wealth of ancient plant and animal life at the site were part of a well-watered oasis existing in an otherwise dry grassland environment during ancient Vero's Ice Age. All of which would have drawn some of Florida's first people to this location," Andy Hemmings, who works there now, told the TCP News a few years earlier in 2016.

Monte Verde, Chile

One of the most thoroughly scrutinized OTC sites in South America is Monte Verde, located in southern Chile. Monte Verde is thirty-six miles inland from the Pacific Ocean, and eight thousand miles south of the Bering Strait. The site was discovered in 1975 when local farmers brought a veterinary student to look at some strange animal bones they had found. The student contacted Tom Dillehay, now of Vanderbilt University, who was working in Chile at the time. Two years later Dillehay began an excavation of the site, which had been covered by an anaerobic peat bog, preventing air from penetrating. The bog provided incredible preservation of perishable materials. Wooden planks, baskets, marine algae, and other things were pulled from the muck. Radiocarbon dating of bones and charcoal in 1982 gave the site deposits an average date of 14,800 years ago, more than a thousand years older than Clovis. The antiquity of Monte Verde was highly controversial among archaeologists until a group of specialists from around the world came to view the evidence for themselves in 1997. All came away convinced of the site's authenticity. Since then, charcoal from an even lower level at Monte Verde has been dated to 33,000 years ago, but many are skeptical of that extreme age.

Monte Verde upset the theoretical apple cart for many archaeologists in 1982. If people were living in wooden houses and wearing clothing made of hides in southern Chile by 14,800 years ago, how did they get there and where did they come from? Glaciers would have still choked the corridor from the Bering Strait, so they couldn't have come that way. It is suggested that perhaps they came by boat. The people were clearly marine fishers, hunters, and gatherers for their livelihood. But where did they come from? The stone tools at Monte Verde look nothing like Clovis manufacture, so where did that technology originate? Researchers are still trying to answer these questions, but for now, at least some people are convinced there must have been a sea route to South America long before people came over the Bering Land Bridge.

Tom Williams thinks there must be far more regionalization in the archaeological record than we've previously believed. The way he sees it, humans must have come to the Americas in several waves, probably by several different routes, rather than one migration through the Bering Strait. "Technology doesn't change overnight," he says. "We should see signs of development as we go along."

"But unless you are looking for it," adds Clark, "and know what to look for, you won't see it. You have to look for old dirt and old context."

Evidence from other sites has also challenged the Clovis First model. Several hypotheses, or ideas about how things work, have been proposed to answer the questions of how, when, and where men and women first came to the Western Hemisphere. Some archaeologists, but certainly not all, believe that since older than Clovis sites are found so far apart, and so much older than thirteen thousand years ago, Ice Age immigrants must have come from different places at different times.

David Meltzer, professor of anthropology at Southern Methodist University, suggested three criteria by which to judge the pre-Clovis antiquity of a site in his book *First Peoples in a New World: Colonizing Ice Age America*: "1) undeniable traces of humans, either their artifacts or skeletal remains, in 2) undisturbed geological deposits in proper stratigraphic position, which are, 3) accompanied by indisputable radiometric ages." Gault has plenty of artifacts undeniably made by humans, and according to Mike Collins and geoarchaeologist Charles Frederick, remarkably undisturbed geologic deposits in the proper sequence of layers, or stratigraphy. Optically stimulated luminescence is returning dates with high degrees of consistency, although some archaeologists would prefer to see radiocarbon dates instead. Radiocarbon dating requires charcoal, preferably in good context, like a hearth or fire pit. Unfortunately, organic materials suitable for dating are not preserved in the early deposits at Gault. Nonetheless, the emerging Gault data seem to hold great promise for anchoring a new paradigm concerning the earliest peopling of the Americas.

6 Problems, Setbacks, and Obstacles

Any long-term outdoor project, whether it is high-rise construction or archaeology, encounters certain obstacles and setbacks from time to time. Gault was no exception. The archaeologists who were there experienced flash floods and torrential rain, high ground water seeping into the pits, extreme temperatures, disruptive visits by film crews and news media, cows, snakes, and accidents. But the first problem Mike faced after walking the site in 1991 was getting permission to come back.

Land and Permission

Nealy Lindsey's estate owned the land at that time, and Elmer, his son, was not particularly keen on archaeologists. He had heard rumors from artifact collectors that archaeologists would keep everything they found and take his land. He was also making money via a pay-to-dig scheme, which of course he didn't want to lose. So when Tom Hester approached him about digging some test pits, Elmer was hesitant. At last, he decided that Tom could bring a crew out for a couple of weeks, but only if he paid the going price.

Normally archaeologists don't pay landowners to excavate on their property. Most archaeology in the United States today is conducted by independent businesses (cultural resource consultants) or government agencies such as the Texas Department of Transportation. In 1966 the United States passed a law requiring archaeological investigation on land that would be permanently impacted by federally funded highway or other construction, such as building dams. Other research is performed by universities, such as Texas State University, typically funded by private donations or scientific grants.

Tom and his colleague Mike were perplexed by the situation with Lindsey. After several weeks of discussion back and forth, a benefactor decided to finance the operation for the university. That gave Hester and Collins twelve days from May 20 to June 1, 1991, to test the area near Buttermilk Creek for evidence of ancient human occupation. They found more than 91,500 artifacts, mostly chert flakes, which was not unusual for Central Texas sites. They knew they had something big, but what? When their contract was up, Mr. Lindsey went back to collecting money for an afternoon of treasure hunting, and the archaeologists lost access to the land.

"Collins got a lot of flack at UT for working with Lindsey," said Jon Lohse, who is now a member of the GSAR board. "But Mike is a man of commitment and vision. This was an impressive lesson. Mike made a career-scale commitment. He could see what could happen by taking a long-term view and making that commitment."

A number of Mike's colleagues at the time were dead set against ever paying a landowner for the right to excavate. Many were afraid such an arrangement would justify commodification of cultural artifacts, such as we see when looters sell arrowheads or ancient statues on the open market. In the early twentieth century, museums throughout Europe and America often purchased materials this way. For example, the Metropolitan Museum of Art in New York purchased a stolen sixth-century BCE Greek vase in 1972. After years of controversy, however, the pot was finally returned to Greece in 2009.

Further, many archaeologists argue against paying a landowner to dig because that would boost the market value of materials that were already in circulation among collectors. Professionals do not want to encourage further destruction of archaeological sites by diggers just wanting to make a buck.

Archaeologists do not sell or trade artifacts. They make no money from their discoveries. Even if somebody writes a book about a discovery, it rarely makes money. Tom and Mike knew all this, of course. When is it OK to cross an arbitrary boundary in the name of science? They wrestled with the dilemma and took a chance. Mike's goal was larger than any monetary transaction, so he tried to accomplish as much as possible those few days in 1991.

Finally, in 1998, they gained entry again after Elmer sold the property to a developer, and his nephew Howard and his son Ricky convinced him to buy a piece back. They had just found the mammoth mandible and called Collins to return. Collins and Lundelius, the UT Austin paleontologist, returned to the site on August 1, 1998, with twelve volunteers to excavate the bones.

After that, excavation at Gault was carried on intermittently from 1999 to 2002. When the agreement with the landowners came to an end, the Lindseys decided not to renew the contract.

They wanted to build a home on the property instead. After lengthy discussions, however, the family gave Collins an opportunity to purchase the area of archaeological interest on Henry Clay Gault's old farm. Unfortunately, he couldn't raise the needed funding—well over half a million dollars.

The site languished for several years when at last Collins made the decision to purchase the place with his own money. In February 2007 he bought two parcels of about forty acres each, and by the end of the same week, he donated sixty acres to the Archaeological Conservancy, a nonprofit organization dedicated to conserving archaeological sites found on private land. After

The Archaeological Conservancy protects archaeological sites nationwide for long-term preservation.

more than fifteen years of delayed research, Mike finally felt confident that he could finish the scientific job at Gault properly, all the way to the bedrock.

Rain and Water

Rain and water were constant issues at Gault. Because of the high water table near the creek, pumps were going almost every day to keep water out of the excavation pits. Almost as soon as they started testing in 1991, Mike had to set up pumps to keep water out of the square holes. Almost every morning the excavation units had to be pumped out or bailed out by hand. And every night, rain or not, underground water seeped back up to fill the open units. Digging at Gault was a muddy, dirty job. Mike's journal entries for May 1991 tell a story that continued in various ways for twenty-five years:

> **May 25, 1991:** After a brief shower, the rain has held off this morning, but it looks like it could come a deluge any minute.
>
> **May 26, 1991:** Arrived at +/– 8:10, began immediately to dewater with 2 pumps and bucket-bailing. TRH and crew had found the site too wet to get into yesterday am (Sat May 25, 1991) after rain on Friday evening and early Sat am . . .
>
> **May 29, 1991:** Since this is slowly rising ground water, it does no damage while entering the units. It is crystal clear in the units in the mornings. . . . Our major concern today is dewatering as our excavation is almost as deep as our deepest sumps. We need to dig a deeper sump, the problem is where to dig it.

May is usually the wettest month of the year in Central Texas, so some of this was to be expected. Nonetheless, weather can present acute problems for those working out in the field.

Jim Adovasio also visited one day in October 2000 to consult on material coming out of Gault. Unfortunately they got rained out. "Site was muddy when we arrived and it rained while we were there—too muddy for work this weekend and forecast is for heavy rain," noted Mike.

By November there had been so much rain that fall that excavation walls were collapsing, as the dirt just would not hold. Mike wrote in his journal:

Excavation pits would often fill up with clear spring water due to the high water table. Here Sergio Ayala and Charles Koenig prepare for 3D photogrammetry documentation.

The recent rains totally collapsed all of the units in the North field. We have water running through Lindsey pit and standing in Hamster pit and 1018 trench. Buttermilk Creek flowing. Much rain has fallen over the past 5 or 6 weeks, raising the water table and returning Buttermilk Creek to a strongly flowing stream. All open units North of the creek have completely collapsed, water is standing in the Hamster block, most of the units N of creek, and is flowing thru the Lindsey Pit excavations at a rapid clip. Critical excavations are lagging and some damage is occurring.

The following weeks of November saw more of the same.

Nov. 14, 2000: Note: Very heavy rain fell on Thursday according to Howard, at least six inches fell on site. Heavy flooding on Buttermilk Creek (highest Howard has even seen!) Water was around 8 feet deep at creek, according to Howard.

Nov. 25, 2000: There was extensive flooding and running water damage to site and equipment; . . . saw two screens washing downstream. Using debris drift lines, we are able to establish elevation of water at three points along the valley.

. . .

Over the last 3 days, I had to rebuild generator and gasoline pump—these were completely submerged in the flood. Generator had mud and organic debris in [it] but fuel and crankcase were okay. Gasoline pump had water in the cylinder, carburetor, fuel tank and crankcase. After cleaning, drying, and refilling everything, both machines work fine (we had just gotten these back from the shop on the 14th where we spent $300.00 on repairs).

December 19, 2000: Over two weeks of very wet weather has curtailed field work and further damaged areas of the site with erosion of excavation walls, sedimentation and ponding in units and wind disturbance of our plastic coverings.

By the end of May 2001, more than 375 members of the Texas Archeological Society (TAS) had registered to work for a week at Gault. The summer excavation and field school is always a popular event for the group, and is always well attended, even if some folks come only for a day or two. Mike was concerned about the possibility of so many people in the field at once and the strain that would put on supervisors who would be training new arrivals each day. He therefore decided to scale back effort in each excavation area and to eliminate some areas entirely. "This is good in terms of logistics and supervision," he wrote.

By the third day of the field school, Mike had killed another rattlesnake at the water cooler. People were working hard, deep in the Clovis layer, but it was slow going. They were digging with bamboo splints rather than metal trowels to avoid damaging anything they might find.

Most of the families and individuals camped overnight on a nearby ranch, telling stories about howling wolves, and scaring the pants off the newcomers. People were having a good time. Then on day seven, the rain started.

The storm hit with a fury a little before 3:00 a.m. with heavy rain, wind, and lightening. Tents blew down, and bedding got soaked, and lots of people spent the rest of the night cramped up trying to sleep in their cars. In the next three hours, it rained about six inches. "We were completely flooded and washed out," said Bryan Jameson. "All of us were in a state of shock and disbelief."

"I remember the rain pounding down in torrents that night/early morning. My tent held up well, but I put on my knee-high rubber boots in the morning," chimed in Jonelle Miller-Chapman. "Field school always has a weather problem! It wouldn't be a field school if every day were sunny and clear. The weather creates memories, like the time it rained baseball sized hail in Perryton, 2009. It smashed through the roof of a nearby pop-up trailer and landed on the floor! That is scary!" Jonelle recalled.

When Mike surveyed the damage the next morning, he wrote that "rainwater in buckets yielded a consistent estimate ca. [of approximately] 5–5.5 inches. Buttermilk Creek got ca. 3 feet out of its banks. . . . Considerable water flowed down the tributaries and deposited flood debris on the alluvial

Workers sometimes had to jump the creek when rain forced them to leave. Most of the time, people were prepared.

fans. Small fish were stranded on the Buttermilk Creek floodplain. Much flood debris in silt fence along property line. . . . This storm brought to a close TAS FS 2001 excavation with an estimated loss of ~150 person days (Friday and Saturday)."

"Excavation blocks were like little mini-swimming pools. Just horror. Just carnage, standing water everywhere," added Bryan.

Mike scrambled to start the cleanup as the remaining TAS volunteers packed up their things. He asked for photographers to document flood damage and record conditions at each excavation area. He called all block supervisors and key crew chiefs to make an accounting of damage for their area, report the status of any field records or artifact bags left in units, and the condition of the unscreened dirt, some of which washed away.

Another torrential rain in September 2009 created an emergency call for volunteers at Gault to help repair the damage done to excavation units, roads, and paths. There was a "huge collapse of the North Wall including the lower bench," recorded Nancy Williams concerning the unit of deepest Clovis excavation. "The pit was filled at least three or more times to overflow. Initial damage assessment severe to extreme. Overall outcome devastating!!! Prognosis—long term effects from damage and slow recovery. 5–6 months for total recovery." Later she recounted that "using aggressive methods it took approx [sic] 7 days to remove flood muck and re-establish grid area and unit lines. Another 2–3 weeks using aggressive methods to remove sediments until landscape fabric or other non-artifact material found."

Mike continued a few days later: "Site is damaged after heavy rains of more than 4 inches. Huge tree down, damaged road, much erosion. Reportedly we had about 5.5 inches of rain in 30 mins (NWS radar estimate)."

When an archaeological site incurs flooding like this, years of work can be destroyed and irreplaceable cultural artifacts can be lost. It can be as though a car drove through a chemistry laboratory. Things get broken and jumbled, and hours of hard work go down the drain. Mike was prepared for such an event, however. Every evening before the crew quit work, they laid landscaping fabric over every excavated surface to hold materials in place underneath in perfect condition. That way no artifacts were lost, even though considerable damage to the site itself occurred.

Citizen scientists and other volunteers rushed in to help. People came from everywhere, including some who drove six or eight hours from East

Heavy rains could cause extensive damage at Gault. Thick mud kept workers out of the field for days.

Texas and people who drove just twenty-three miles from nearby Fort Hood. They all came to work in the mud pits, shoring up the walls, gathering up equipment that had floated downstream, and cleaning up the mess.

There were other encounters with Fort Hood from time to time, May Schmidt related. Fort Hood, the largest active duty armored post in the US Military Services, is only a short distance away from the Gault site. "We could actually hear artillery practice sometimes. Once a building in Killeen was hit by live ammunition by mistake. The colonel had to come out to the landowner and apologize."

Wouldn't you know, the next September it wasn't artillery—it was another flood. As Mike said:

Sept. 8, 2010: Today is 362 days after the deluge of 9–11–09 damage to our Area 15 excavation. That rain event was 5.5 inches of rain in 30 mins. The 2010 event measured 11 or 12 inches in about 14–15 hours (based on our 11 inch rain gauge being absolutely filled and 12 inches in an empty bucket left outside the tent.

Bluebonnets, purple verbena, and yellow daisies paint the meadows at Gault each spring.

"We had so much rain," said May Schmidt, "and we were down in a little valley, along the creek. If we heard thunder, someone would say, 'I sure hope that's heavy artillery!'"

Nature continued to have her way at the Gault site, as she always does. Once Bruce Bradley's group was "chased out early by a violent storm that moved in from the west. Lots of lightning, heavy rain, and a tornado down between Leander and Georgetown." A few days later, they "returned to camp to find tent blown down. Fun putting it back up in the dark with gale-force winds." Violent storms are well-known in Central Texas, with 244 tornadoes recorded in the state in 2015.

Heat and Cold

It was the heat that was dangerous, however, in the summer of 2009. On June 27, Boy Scouts came to visit, and Mike noted:

> **June 27, 2009:** Yesterday and today extremely hot: 108 degrees F and above in Weatherport [an all-weather tent erected over Area 15]. Up to 114 in Weatherport yesterday. Buttermilk Creek is dry over about the upper half of its length across the A. C. property. Still finding some evidence of looters in upper ~30 cm of the 1079 line.

As summer dragged on, he commented:

> **July and August 2009:** Severe water shortage leads to very limited water screening. Although upper part of creek is dry, ~100 m downstream . . . springs are present in creek bed. This is in accord with historic and oral historic accounts that say even in driest years there is a little flow in this part of the creek.

But Mike had a weather protocol the team followed. Sharon Dornheim explained: "We didn't go out if it was raining or below thirty-two degrees. Mike and I would be on the phone at 4:00 a.m. debating the weather because we had to meet students and volunteers at TARL [Texas Archeological Research Lab] at 6:00 a.m."

Volunteers from New Hampshire sported new jackets during a March snowstorm at Gault. The Weatherport over Area 15 is behind them.

There were only a few days when the team stayed home because of cold. On December 5, 2009, Mike recorded that it was "19 degrees F in the barn at 8 AM. Too cold to water screen." Water screening involves washing buckets of dirt through very fine screen mesh in order to recover tiny fragments of shell, bone, rock, and so forth. Archaeologists do this by hand, using keen observation to spot any tiny bit. The crew was probably grateful to be doing something else that day.

News Media

Because the discoveries about ancient man at Gault were so amazing, media personnel were often around filming or scribbling notes about the site. Crews from CNN, National Geographic, *Scientific American Frontiers* from PBS, Korean TV, and others frequented the site to report on the latest old news of thirteen thousand years ago. Once a German film crew "spent a full

Alan Alda questions Mike Collins about stone tools during the filming of the TV show *Scientific American Frontiers* for PBS.

day filming areas of the site, [gathering] interviews regarding the site and its artifacts, and [walking through] the scene of excavation activities," Mike explained. After that, Mike and the German crew returned to the lab in Austin and filmed until almost 11:00 p.m. "This turned out to be about a nineteen-hour day for me," he admitted.

Other times, cameras, lights, and microphones, in addition to numerous excavation pits of varying depths, created a tricky maze within which the archaeological crew had to maneuver. Print reporters for local newspapers, glossy magazines, and others often visited as well. Wonderful as such publicity is, each time media folks came to the site, Mike was pulled away to guide them around. Admittedly it's a nice problem to have, but sometimes TV cameras and microphones can get in the way of regular work. Mike spent many hectic days explaining what the archaeology team was doing, what they were finding, and what it all meant.

Accidents

There were only two serious accidents during the work at Gault. One was a broken wrist, caused by stumbling on steps into a deep hole. The other was a strangulated hernia caused by heavy jolting on a Bobcat excavator. Mike went to the hospital with that one—the long, slow, and painful way.

One thing that archaeologists worry about is having an accident in some remote location where help is hard to get. Even though the Gault site is only a few miles from the nearest small town, and about twenty miles to a fairly good-sized one, during the period of excavation out there, there was no cell phone service to call for help quickly. And the tangle of country roads to get there would be a nightmare to describe to EMS in an emergency.

He'd been slamming the excavator into mounds of dirt when suddenly he felt a pain. He stopped and got off, and knew he was in trouble. And old hernia had reopened. Quickly and quietly, without any fanfare, he cancelled work for the rest of the day and commandeered someone to drive him into Austin. This was about 2:00 p.m. He was pale and vomiting by the time he got to the hospital, after a stop or two along the way at his request. By 6:00 p.m. he was taken immediately into surgery. The crew held their breath while he was in the hospital, but within a few days he was released, fully on the mend, and things got back to normal.

Heat, Cows, and Snakes

In June 2000, archaeology students from Brigham Young University under the direction of Joel Janetski came to work at Gault for their field school requirement. One of them wrote that "it seems that the heat and humidity are getting to people, and making [them] slightly crazy." Several people suffered from heat stroke from time to time, and people could get cranky. Besides the Texas heat, another pointed out, "in addition to the water issues on site, there are also grazing and livestock concerns. Since cattle have been allowed to graze in the pasture where the excavations are taking place, it is probably necessary to setup some fencing. [Someone] has been enlisted to gather all available orange fencing (which will at some point presumably be placed around the excavation area)."

"Cow TV" amused workers in the Weatherport. Critics said the characters and scenery were great, but the plot was rather slow.

By the next day, fencing had been put up and the cows seemed to be happily grazing on the other side. Then, some days later, several curious bovines broke through the fence and had to be herded up again. This went on for several days: crew puts up the fence; cows break through the fence; crew rounds up the cows; cows pretend to be content until the crew leaves and then waltz right through the fence again. Fortunately no severe damage was done to the site or the crew or the animals themselves through these shenanigans. In fact, the bucolic bovines provided a bit of relief, through what became known as "Cow TV."

A huge tent, known rather grandly as a Weatherport, had been erected over an important area of deep Clovis excavation. This tent had several windows, which could be rolled up to admit the cross-breeze, if any existed. When people would raise up, bamboo knife in hand, to rest their backs for a moment, or grab another bucket, occasionally they would see beautiful gold and white longhorns strolling by through the window. Not much, but it passed for entertainment.

Snakes were not as welcome, however. Once Clark was walking with a visitor when they heard a little squeak. "What's that?" asked the guest. Then they saw it: a snake with its jaws around a little mouse. Out in the country, there are going to be snakes, and at least three rattlers were caught and/or killed the summer of 2000. "We had a water moccasin show up at the site," commented James Beers. "I found it and Dr. Janetski disposed of it with a shovel. I've never seen a snake move that fast; it was like lightning. Freaky!" Collins doubts the snake was a water moccasin, however, saying it was probably a nonpoisonous diamond-backed water snake instead. Nonetheless, it made people jump. Numerous other snakes were dispatched for the workers' comfort.

Archaeologists and others who work outdoors must take all these things in stride, however. Rain, heat, and cold are ever present. Animals can run through fences or chew up materials left unprotected. Accidents are always a concern in any occupation. These incidents delay work and cost money, but generally Mike and his team were well prepared. On a long-term project such as Gault, weather and delays are inevitable, but not crippling. The work continued as long as permission and persistence allowed.

Catch of the day from the Lindsey pit, May 7, 2002. These are probably non-poisonous diamondback water snakes. Although they are not venomous, they do bite. Project personnel generally recorded and left wildlife alone, but these had rather aggressively taken over an active excavation.

7 Conclusion

Mike leaned back in his chair at his office and looked at a cast of the "hotdog in a bun" that David Olmstead found. "That certainly set us off on a chase," he said dryly, "but there's still a lot more work to do." As more sites with the right kind of dirt are analyzed, more evidence of the earliest occupation of the Americas will certainly be discovered. "One of the problems is that we have to learn to recognize the subtle indicators of older than Clovis material," said Mike. "And in order to do that, we have to broaden our mind-sets to include a whole range of what might be possible. After all, we usually only find what we're looking for."

Almost one hundred professional members of the Society for American Archeology (SAA) saw Gault for themselves in separate trips in 2007 and 2014. They were in Austin both years for the annual meeting of the SAA, and had heard Mike and others present their Gault findings at the meeting. About sixty-five took a bus from Austin to see the site in 2007. They tumbled out of the bus and walked across the uplands in the warm spring sun. Several took off their jackets and put on sunglasses. By the time they got to the excavation area they had come to see, more than one were gently perspiring.

"What've you got here, Mike?" one said.

"Well come on in and I'll show you," he responded. Archaeologists stood around the open pit so everyone could get a good view of the stratigraphy, or layers of soil that were above what Mike hoped would be the Clovis layer.

By 2014, the pit was open all the way to bedrock, and Mike knew undoubtedly that he had Clovis, and something more. The crowd stood around the top, and Mike climbed down the stairs, talking and pointing as he went. "You can see here's where the Clovis layer starts," he said, pointing at a dark, deep band of soil. People asked a few questions, but mostly they were interested in what lay below the Clovis layer. "Right here, this yellow layer, is a largely barren deposit of gritty clay alluvium, fifteen centimeters thick. Now this stratum here has the potential to date older than Clovis." The compacted soil was also alluvium, but with less clay.

"Well, what do you think?" asked Mike.

"I'd say you've got something interesting here," said one of the group members. A few others nodded.

"Can I come down and take a look?" someone asked.

"Sure," said Mike. "Come on down. Careful, there."

The other archaeologist bent his head to look closely at the perfectly straight, scraped wall. He touched his finger to a bit of chert poking out and shined his flashlight on it. He asked a question or two, and then dusted off his hands and climbed back up.

Members of the Society for American Archeology (SAA) overlook Area 15, where Clovis and older than Clovis artifacts were found in a 2014 visit. Mike Collins is at the bottom of the stairs.

"What about mixing?" one person asked, concerned about the possibility of artifacts being displaced in the soil by various means.

"That's why I wanted you to come out here," replied Mike. "You tell me. What do you see?"

A few onlookers shifted their weight to get a better view.

"Anybody else?" asked Mike. "Well, if there're no more questions here, let's head up to the barn."

The group trooped down the path, across the creek, and up the slope to the weathered farm building where about two hundred tools, flakes, and slivers of chert were laid out on a table. They gathered around and picked up certain pieces here and there. They looked carefully at the edges of the stones to see how they were broken. Mike talked about the technical aspects he had noted in the way the chips were fashioned. He answered a few pointed questions. Somebody grunted, but nobody contradicted the conviction that this was unusually old material.

SAA members view Clovis and older than Clovis artifacts displayed in the barn at Gault. Members discussed the merits of the discoveries and possible problems with interpretation.

Critics and Other Views

It would take years of analysis in the lab to determine conclusively what these stone fragments were. Sophisticated dating methods would have to be applied. Use-wear analysis would have to be done. Starch grain analysis would be employed. But during two brief visits to the site, some of the best archaeologists in America seemed to agree that Gault was something special.

Of course, some critics continue to be skeptical of any older than Clovis claims. For example, Jared Diamond, author of *Guns, Germs and Steel*, wrote that "if there really had been pre-Clovis settlement, we would already know it and would no longer be arguing about it. That's because there would now be hundreds of undisputed pre-Clovis sites distributed everywhere from the Canada/U.S. border south to Chile." Juliet Morrow and Stuart Fiedel also question artifacts claimed to be older than Clovis, such as those at the Friedkin site and Monte Verde. They caution that objects (especially those near a stream bed) can be moved by water, tree roots, or animals, and that more distinct features need to be identified before researchers can be assured of pre-Clovis dates.

Too few older than Clovis sites have been investigated to make generalizations about what the stone artifacts or any other remains might look like or how we might recognize them. Other issues such as natural mixing of soils, contamination of samples, and accurate dating continue to be evaluated.

Area 15 at Gault was completely backfilled in January 2015, and all excavation halted. There was no further to go since they had hit bedrock. In a few decades, if new technologies are developed, the unit could always be expanded again with the purpose of recovering more data. But until then, the dirt protects the secrets of human life from thousands of years ago.

The discoveries of unmistakable traces of human handiwork prior to the Clovis cultural period pose more questions than answers. If humans were in both North and South America prior to the development of Clovis technology, where did they come from? How did they get here, and when did they arrive? How can scientists recognize the remnants they might have left behind?

Dennis Stanford of the National Museum of Natural History at the Smithsonian Institution and Bruce Bradley have proposed a North Atlantic route to the East Coast of North America, based on similarities of certain stone tools found at Cactus Hill in Virginia and other sites along the Atlantic coast to those from France and Spain more than twenty thousand years ago. Boats made of hides might have carried people along frozen Atlantic pack ice "coastline," affording them fresh water from melting ice and allowing them to catch fish and seals along the way. It seems possible that people could have paddled along the pack ice that existed from the coast of what is now France all the way to the Western Hemisphere during the last glacial maximum. These brave adventurers could have hauled out on ice floes to obtain fresh water from snow melt and shelter during the night or in storms. They could have used seal blubber for fuel. And it is possible that some might have settled somewhere along the Atlantic seaboard of North America as they expanded their maritime fishing and hunting territory.

In contrast to a North Atlantic route, a Pacific coastal route is now widely accepted, albeit the timing is still debated. A Pacific coastal route was first proposed in 1979 by Knut Fladmark. The Pacific shoreline extended ten to thirty miles further west during the Ice Age than it currently does. If early pioneers came along this route in boats, it is possible that older than Clovis materials lie submerged under the sea, awaiting discovery. It is also possible that some of these explorers could have paddled and walked down the coast of South America and finally settled in Monte Verde, Chile, only a few miles inland. The ancestors of the first people to camp at Gault could have reached North America by boat, and then walked inland, perhaps for several generations, to the south-central part of the continent.

"It is important that we have an understanding of the dispersal of human beings across the planet, how we survived certain conditions using culture, so that we can add to the story of what it means to be human as a whole to reduce the divisions among us," said Charles Speer, Assistant Professor and Curator of Anthropology at the Idaho Museum of Natural History at Idaho State University.

We are only now beginning to understand human migration patterns to the New World. No matter where the first people in the Americas came from, or how they got here, scientists know for sure that Gault and other sites present evidence of robust Clovis-age populations and perhaps earlier habitation by as yet unknown groups.

Tamra Walter from Texas Tech University chimed in. "Gault is important because the prehistoric record is finite. There just aren't many of these sites.

The antiquity at Gault is tremendous. Also the material culture there is exceptional. People need to know about the ancient past [to understand] the time depth for how long people have been around and to appreciate what humans are capable of, and that even though they may have lived ten thousand years ago, they were human, just like us. People [today] need to become good stewards of the past."

"Gault has revealed an exceptional record of the human experience in a rich ecotonal environment, from the earliest known occupations in the region to contact with Euro-American societies. The Clovis record is especially rich in information," commented Bruce Bradley.

Jon Lohse predicts the impact Gault will make on the history of the Americas "will be vast, especially in terms of education, training, and overall understanding of human beings on this continent."

"Gault is important because it provides us with an opportunity to expand what we thought we knew about the peopling of the continent," added Sharon Dornheim. "It's an artifact rich location with so much potential for us to see beyond what we already knew and understood."

Pam Wheat Stranahan explained that it's important for ordinary people to know about the past because of "human curiosity. People wonder how other people lived. It's important to develop at sense of place. That's what archaeology and history do for you. Gault is important because you can see the continuum of time as well as different human adaptations."

Growing DNA research seems to indicate that Native Americans are descended from Asian stock, thus bolstering the Pacific coastal route theory. Recent DNA studies indicate that Native Americans diverged from their Asian ancestors about twenty-five thousand years ago, and perhaps lived along the Bering Land Bridge during that time before venturing further south. DNA evidence for early Native American ancestry is quite limited, however, and remains inconclusive. For instance, we have only one example of DNA from a Clovis-era individual from the Ansick site in Montanta. Other burials of that age simply have not been found. No examples of human remains earlier than the Clovis period have been recovered.

There is still much to study in this regard. No matter how human beings arrived in the Western Hemisphere, or what route they took, scientists are gaining clarity on early populations thanks to thousands of modern people working together to recover the past.

"What is now clear is that there were many peoples in the Americas before Clovis and we face the task of learning how these cultural-historical pieces fit together," Mike wrote in 2014. The pleasant place near the bubbling creek in Central Texas has been inviting people to visit for short periods or many years throughout the millennia. The people passing by have left scraps of their daily lives behind for us to find and ponder. The new questions that arise from this quest to find the past will occupy archaeologists and citizen scientists for many years to follow.

Conclusion

Clovis is well-known from many archaeological sites across North America and sparsely down the spine of the continents to northern Venezuela. From its early recognition in the mid-1930s, Clovis has held a special place in the hearts and minds of archaeologists. One version of that special niche holds that Clovis represented traces left by the first settlers in the Americas. This is in spite of the extremely widespread distribution of Clovis evidence, which makes it unlikely that Clovis could represent the first peopling of the hemisphere. Even so, this "Clovis First" idea became so embedded in archaeological thinking that when evidence for earlier human presence came to light, the controversial concept of "pre-Clovis" arose. In its worst sense, this term was used pejoratively to refer to evidence of people here in times prior to Clovis and was generally meant to dismiss such findings. In a more positive sense, "pre-Clovis" was used to promote new and interesting findings like those at Cactus Hill or Monte Verde. For years archaeologists have squabbled as to whether this find or that is "pre-Clovis," simply indicating it is older than Clovis, or that it is "proto-Clovis," meaning that it is both older than Clovis *and* ancestral to Clovis, thus serving as a prototype from which Clovis stone technology was developed.

Collins has an inkling that in the millennia leading up to the advent of Clovis there were many, diverse groups of people spreading and settling across the landscape. He has identified seven patterns in older than Clovis sites in North America that demonstrate this idea. He is not alone in this view and has recently written that not only do we have a number of sites in the Americas that are older than Clovis, but that those sites can be arrayed into archaeological patterns—multiple sites of similar age and composed of

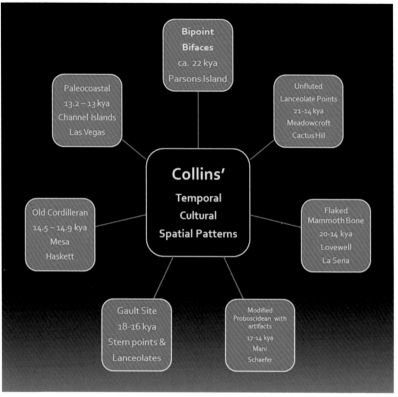

Mike Collins believes seven patterns exist in the currently known data for older than Clovis in the Americas. Archaeologists look for patterns to help interpret sites. (Adapted from Collins et al. 2014.)

similar evidence over a variety of temporal and spatial areas. Archaeology relies heavily on patterning in evidence. Two similar sites are more convincing than a single one, and confidence increases as the numbers of sites sharing the same traits rises.

Collins's Patterns of Possible Older than Clovis

The first pattern in Collins's scheme consists of one main site and eleven other possible locations along the East Coast of North America where large distinctive thin laurel leaf bifaces have been found. Dating for these objects suggests an interval of approximately twenty-two thousand years ago. A good example of this pattern is the Parsons Island site near Chesapeake Bay.

Also along the Atlantic seaboard are four sites manifesting unfluted lanceleolate points and prismatic blades. These compose the second pattern. Dates for these sites range between fourteen and twenty-one thousand years ago. The two best known of this group are Meadowcroft Shelter in Pennsylvania and Cactus Hill in Virginia.

Pattern three contains ten sites in the North American grasslands from the Valley of Mexico to the last glacial margins where flaked mammoth bones indicate human activity. These sites appear to date around fourteen to twenty thousand years ago. The Lovewell site in Kansas is part of this group.

The Hebior and Schaefer sites about an hour north of Chicago represent pattern four, which consists of five sites where modified proboscidean bones (such as mammoth or mastodon) occur in association with stone or bone artifacts. These appear to date to about fourteen thousand years ago.

The Gault and Friedkin sites form the fifth of Collins's patterns. They are in the periphery of the Southern Plains and have cultural materials beneath Clovis components, dating to between thirteen to sixteen thousand years ago.

The sixth pattern is seen in numerous sites along the Pacific margins of North and South America. They share the presence of thick, narrow projectile points, but lack microblades. These can be dated to about fourteen thousand years ago, and are known as Old Cordilleran. The Mesa archaeological site in Alaska is a good example.

The last pattern is found on the Channel Islands off California and dates from around 13,200 years ago. Small, stemmed projectile points are the identifying artifacts found here.

From these seven patterns, we can see a good deal of variety. What seemed in earlier thinking to be a rapid spread of a single people across North America in only a few hundred years at the end of the last Ice Age may instead have been the spread of Clovis technology across a host of many different peoples who had already settled over thousands of years into favorable environmental niches from southern Chile through the expanse of North America.

What this array of patterns and the individual sites of which they are composed tell us is that American prehistory had a long and varied run before Clovis times. With this much variety in the archaeological record, the human groups who left evidence of their presence as well as hints of their various lifestyles were probably biologically and culturally diverse. They most likely had multiple belief systems, spoke many languages, and survived using many distinct practices. This story also bumps Clovis from its vaulted place as America's first culture to a place perhaps near the middle of at least thirty thousand years of American human history (considering the earliest component at Monte Verde, Chile, is dated to thirty-three thousand years ago). The first half of this history is very poorly known, and a vast amount of research effort will be needed to more fully document and interpret that history. Countless exciting new finds and many surprises undoubtedly will punctuate this research, so archaeologists and others will have much to do in the future.

The Gault site has contributed much to the current understanding of Clovis culture and provides tantalizing hints of what came before. Today, walking along the creek, visitors see no trace of excavation, as everything has been backfilled with dirt and overgrown with vegetation. A few explanatory signs erected by GSAR along the way describe the work of Collins and others, and periodic tours present the opportunity for a nice walk in the country. Except for the signs, the scene looks much as it would have when Henry Gault bought the land. The water gurgles and the birds chirp, guarding the secrets of ages past.

Further Reading

Adovasio, J. M., and David Pedler. 2016. *Strangers in a New Land: What Archaeology Reveals about the First Americans*. Buffalo, NY: Firefly Books.

Adovasio, J. M., with Jake Page. 2002. *The First Americans: In Pursuit of Archaeology's Greatest Mystery*. New York: Random House.

Begley, Janet. 2018. "Old Vero Man Not as Old as Originally Thought after Archaeologists Analyze Artifacts." *TCPalm*, April 9, 2018, https://www.tcpalm.com/story/news/local indian-river-county/2018/04/09/old-vero-man-not-old-originally-thought-after-archaeologists-analyze-artifacts. Accessed April 23, 2018.

Bousman, C. Britt, Barry W. Baker, and Anne C. Kerr. 2004. "Paleoindian Archeology in Texas." In *The Prehistory of Texas*, edited by Timothy K. Perttula. Texas A&M University Anthropology Series 9. College Station: Texas A&M University Press.

Bradley, Bruce. 1999. "Clovis Ivory and Bone Tools." http://www.primtech.net/ivory/ivory.html. Accessed August 30, 2016. Reprinted from J. Hahn, M. Menu, Y. Taboren, P. Walter, and F. Widemann, eds., *Le Travail et L'usage de l'invoire au Paleolithique Superieur*. Ravello: Instituto Poligrafico e Zecca dello Stato Liberia dello Stato.

Bradley, Bruce A., Michael B. Collins, and C. Andrew Hemmings, with contributions by Marilyn Shoberg and Jon C. Lohse. 2010. *Clovis Technology*. Archeological Series 17. Ann Arbor: International Monographs in Prehistory.

Cole, Melanie. 1993. "Engraved in Stone." *Texas Monthly*, January 1993, 72–73.

Collins, Michael B. 2014. "Initial Peopling of the Americas: Context, Findings and Issues." In *Cambridge World Prehistory*, vol. 3, edited by Colin Renfrew and Paul G. Bahn. Cambridge: Cambridge University Press.

———. 2007. "Discerning Clovis Subsistence from Stone Artifacts and Site Distributions on the Southern Plains Periphery." In *Foragers of the Terminal Pleistocene in North America*, edited by Renee B. Walker and Boyce N. Driskell. Lincoln: University of Nebraska Press.

————. 2004. "Archaeology of Central Texas." In *The Prehistory of Texas*, edited by Timothy K. Perttula. Texas A&M University Anthropology Series 9. College Station: Texas A&M University Press.

————. 2002. "The Gault Site, Texas, and Clovis Research." *Athena Review* 3 (2): 31–40, 100–101.

Collins, Michael B., T. R. Hester, D. Olmstead, and P. J. Headrick. 1991. "Engraved Cobbles from Early Archeological Contexts in Central Texas." *Current Research in the Pleistocene* 8, 13–15.

Collins, Michael B., Dennis J. Stanford, Darrin L. Lowery, and Bruce Bradley. 2014. "North America before Clovis: Variance in Temporal/Spatial Cultural Patterns 27,000–13,000 cal yr BP." In *Paleoamerican Odyssey*, edited by K. E. Graf, C. V. Ketron, and M. R. Waters. College Station: Texas A&M University Press.

Dillahay, Tom D., Carlos Ocampo, Jose Saavadedra, Andre Oliveira Sawakuchi, Rodrigo M. Vega, and Mario Pino. 2015. "New Archaeological Evidence for an Early Human Presence at Monte Verde, Chile," *PLOS One* 10 (11): 1–27.

Dillay, Tom D. 1984. "A Late Ice-Age Settlement in Southern Chile." *Scientific American* 251 (4): 106–17.

Fladmark, K. 1979. "Routes: Alternate Migration Corridors for Early Man in North America." *American Antiquity* 44 (1): 55–69.

Hester, Thomas R., ed. 1998. *TARL Research Notes*. Volume 6. Austin: University of Texas at Austin, Texas Archeological Research Laboratory.

Hoffecker, John F., Scott A. Elias, and Dennis H. O'Rourke. 2014. "Out of Beringia?" *Science* 343 (6174): 979–80.

Graf, Kelly E., Caroline V. Ketron, and Michael R. Waters, eds. 2014. *Paleoamerican Odyssey*. College Station: Texas A&M University Press.

Gruhn, R. 1988. "Linguistic Evidence in Support of the Coastal Route of Earliest Entry into the New World." *Man* 23 (1; new series): 77–100.

Lancy, David F. 2017. *Raising Children: Surprising Insights from Other Cultures*. Cambridge: Cambridge University Press.

Lemke, Ashley K., D. Clark Wernecke, and Michael B. Collins. 2015. "Early Art in North America: Clovis and Later Paleoindian Incised Artifacts from the Gault Site, Texas (41BL 323)." *American Antiquity* 80 (1): 113–33.

Meltzer, David J. 2009. *First Peoples in a New World: Colonizing Ice EXH Age America*. Berkeley: University of California Press.

Meltzer, David J., Donald K. Grayson, Gerardo Ardila, Alex W. Barker, Dena F. Dincause, C. Vance Haynes. 1997. "On the Pleistocene Antiquity of Monte Verde, Southern Chile." *American Antiquity* 62 (4): 659–63.

Morrow, Juliet E., Stuart J. Fiedel, Donald L. Johnson, Marcel Kornfeld, Moye Rutledge, Raymond Wood. 2012. "Pre-Clovis in Texas? A Critical Assessment of the Buttermilk Creek Complex." *Journal of Archaeological Science* 39 (12): 3677–82.

Morton, Mary Caperton. 2017. "The First Americans: How and When Were the Americas Populated?" *Earth*, January 1, 2017, http://www.earthmagazine.org.

Noble, John Wilford. 2011. "Spear Points Found in Texas Dial Back Arrival of Humans in America." *New York Times*, March 24, 2011, http://www.nytimes.com/2011/03/25/science/25archeo.html.

Oppenheimer, S., Bruce Bradley, and Dennis Stanford. 2014. "Solutrean Hypothesis: Genetics, the Mammoth in the Room." *World Archaeology* 46 (5): 55–63.

Paris, Beverly S. 2016. "Archaeologist Andy Hemmings to Speak April 2 at the Emerson Center." *TCPalm*, March 26, 2016, https://www.tcpalm.com/story/specialty-publications/luminaries/indian-river-county/2016/03/24/archaeologist-andy-hemmings-to-speak-april-2-at-the-emerson-center/89327696/. Accessed February 6, 2018.

Stanford, Dennis J., and Bruce A. Bradley. 2012. *Across Atlantic Ice: The Origins of America's Clovis Culture*. Berkeley: University of California Press.

Texas beyond History. 2005. "Kincaid Shelter: 13,000 Years in the Sabinal River Valley." http://www.texasbeyondhistory.net/kincaid/index.html. Accessed May 24, 2016.

———. 2005. "Plateaus and Canyonlands: Prehistory." http://www.texasbeyondhistory.net/plateaus/prehistory/index.html. Accessed April 16, 2016.

———. 2010. "Horn Shelter: A Paleoindian Grave." http://www.texasbeyondhistory.net/horn/burials.html. Accessed September 3, 2016.

Turner, Ellen Sue, Thomas R. Hester, and Richard L. McReynolds. 2011. *Stone Artifacts of Texas Indians*. 3rd edition. Langham, MD: Taylor Trade Publishing.

Waters, Michael R., Steven L. Forman, Thomas A. Jennings, et al. 2011. "The Buttermilk Creek Complex and the Origins of Clovis at the Debra L. Friedkin Site, Texas." *Science* 331 (6024): 1599–1603.

Wernecke, D. Clark. n.d. *Gault Site History*. Manuscript in progress.

———. 2015. "Lines of Evidence: Early Paleoindian Mobiliary Art in the Americas." Paper presented at the IFRAO Congress, Université d'Extremadura, Cáceres, Spain, August 2015.

Wernecke, D. Clark, and Michael B. Collins. 2010. "Patterns and Process: Some Thoughts on the Incised Stones from the Gault Site, Central Texas, United States." Paper presented at the IFRAO Congress Pleistocene Art of the Word, Tarascon-sur-Ariège and Foix, France, September 2010.

Williams, T. J., N. Velchoff, M. B. Collins, and B. A. Bradley. n.d. "Stone Tool Technology at the Gault Site: Exploring Technology, Patterns, and the Early Human Occupation of North America." In *People and Culture in Ice Age Americas: New Directions in Paleoamerican Archaeology*, edited by R. Suarez and A. Ardelean. Salt Lake City: University of Utah Press.

Zimmer, Carl. 2015. "New Study Links Kennewick Man to Native Americans." *New York Times*, June 19, 2015, A-14.

Index